DR. JEKYLL AND MR. HYDE

NOTES

including
- *Life of the Author*
- *General Plot Summary*
- *List of Characters*
- *Summaries and Critical Commentaries*
- *Character Analyses*
- *Questions for Review*
- *Essay Topics*
- *Select Bibliography*

by
James L. Roberts, Ph.D.
Department of English
University of Nebraska

Wiley Publishing, Inc.

About the Author
James L. Roberts, Ph.D., Department of English, University of Nebraska

Composition
Wiley Indianapolis Composition Services

CliffsNotes™ *Dr. Jekyll and Mr. Hyde*

Published by:
Wiley Publishing, Inc.
111 River Street
Hoboken, NJ 07030
www.wiley.com

Copyright © 1989 Wiley Publishing, Inc., New York, New York
ISBN: 0-8220-0408-9

10
1V/TQ/QZ/QW/IN
Published simultaneously in Canada

CONTENTS

DR. JEKYLL AND MR. HYDE
Notes

LIFE OF THE AUTHOR

Robert Louis Balfour Stevenson was born at Edinburgh, Scotland, on November 13, 1850. He was a sickly youth, and an only son, for whom his parents had high hopes. When at last Stevenson was able to attend school, he did extremely well and entered the university at sixteen. His family expected him to become a lighthouse engineer, a family profession, but Stevenson agreed, as a compromise, to study law instead. He was a young rebel; he thought that his parents' religion was an abomination, and he soon became known as a bohemian, ranting about bourgeois hypocrisy.

When he was twenty-three, Stevenson developed a severe respiratory illness and was sent to the French Riviera to recuperate. This was the first of his many travels abroad, usually to France. In fact, many of his best-known writings use voyages and travels as their framework – *Treasure Island* and *Kidnapped,* for example – and Stevenson would travel for the rest of his life. He was always restless and curious about the world, and he never put down roots for long in any single location.

While Stevenson was staying at Fontainebleau, in France, in 1876 (he was twenty-six), he met Fanny Osbourne, an American woman who was separated from her husband. He fell in love with her, and much to the horror of his parents, he courted her for two years. In 1878, Mrs. Osbourne returned to California, and the elder Stevensons felt that perhaps their son would come to his senses and forget the "loose" American woman. They were wrong. Robert decided to follow Fanny to California. He arrived there in 1879, very ill and very poor. It was not an easy time for the young lovers. Stevenson barely managed to eke out a living and was ill much of the time. They were married early in 1880 and honeymooned on the site of an abandoned silver mine. It was not long, however, before they received a telegram from Stevenson's father, relenting and offering them financial support. Soon afterward, the couple sailed for Scotland.

For some time, the Stevensons lived in Switzerland because of Robert's bad health, but still he continued to suffer from bouts of severe respiratory illness; he returned to the Scottish Highlands, but became critically ill with a lung hemorrhage. He tried living in England, but the climate there was also bad for him. All this time, however, he continued to write and publish. His best-known novels, *Treasure Island* and *Kidnapped,* are both products of this period, as is *The Strange Case of Dr. Jekyll and Mr. Hyde* (1886), more commonly referred to as *Dr. Jekyll and Mr. Hyde.*

In August 1887, Stevenson and his family sailed for America, where he found himself famous. Thus, he chartered a yacht and sailed for the South Seas. He lived there for the rest of his life, writing novels, essays, and poetry and traveling among the islands. *In the South Seas* (1896) and *A Footnote to History* (1892) are records of his fascination with the exotic new peoples and the countries he encountered. Finally, when Stevenson was forty, he decided to make his home in Samoa, and he lived there, with his wife, his mother, and his wife's two children, for four years. He died very suddenly early in December, 1894; surprisingly, his death was due to a cerebral hemorrhage and not to the long-feared tuberculosis which had plagued him so relentlessly throughout his life.

GENERAL PLOT SUMMARY

Every Sunday, Mr. Utterson, a prominent London lawyer, and his distant kinsman, Mr. Richard Enfield, take a stroll through the city of London. Even though to a stranger's eyes, these two gentlemen seem to be complete opposites, both look forward to, and enjoy, their weekly stroll with one another.

One Sunday, they pass a certain house with a door unlike those in the rest of the neighborhood. The door reminds Mr. Enfield of a previous incident in which he witnessed an extremely unpleasant man trampling upon a small, screaming girl while the strange man was in flight from something, or to somewhere. The screams from the small girl brought a large crowd, and various bystanders became incensed with the indifference of the stranger, whose name they discovered to be Mr. Edward Hyde. Enfield can recall the man only with extreme distaste and utter revulsion. The crowd forced the man to make retribution in the form of money, and they were all surprised when he returned from inside the "strange door" with ten pounds in gold and a check for ninety pounds. They held him until the banks opened to make certain that the check was valid because it was signed by the well-known Dr. Henry Jekyll, and they suspected that it was a forgery. To their amazement, the check was valid.

That evening, in his apartment, Mr. Utterson has further reason to be interested in Mr. Hyde because Dr. Jekyll's will has an unusual clause that stipulates that Edward Hyde is to be the sole beneficiary of all of Jekyll's wealth and property. Utterson goes, therefore, to visit an old friend, Dr. Lanyon, who tells him that some ten years ago, he and Dr. Jekyll became estranged because of a professional matter. Utterson decides to seek out Hyde, and he posts himself as a sentinel outside the mysterious door previously mentioned by Enfield. After some time, Utterson encounters the man Hyde entering the door, and he initiates a conversation with him. Hyde suddenly becomes highly suspicious of Utterson's interest in him and quickly retreats inside the door. Utterson walks around the block and knocks at the front door of Dr. Jekyll's house. Upon questioning the butler, Poole, Utterson discovers that Edward Hyde has complete access to Jekyll's house.

About a fortnight later, Utterson is invited to one of Jekyll's dinner parties and remains after the other guests have left so that he can question Jekyll about his will and about his beneficiary, Edward Hyde. Jekyll is unhappy discussing Edward Hyde and insists that his wishes – that Mr. Hyde be the recipient of his property – be honored.

About a year later, an upstairs maid witnesses the vicious murder of a kindly and distinguished old gentleman, the prominent Sir Danvers Carew, M.P. (Member of Parliament). But the assailant escapes before he can be apprehended. The maid, however, is able to positively identify the murderer as Edward Hyde. Mr. Utterson and the police go to Hyde's apartment, but the housekeeper informs them that he is gone. When Utterson confronts Jekyll about the whereabouts of Hyde, Jekyll shows the lawyer a letter which Hyde wrote saying that he was disappearing forever. Jekyll maintains that he himself is completely through with him.

After the disappearance of Hyde, Jekyll comes out of his seclusion and begins a new life, for a time. But at about the same time, Utterson is dining with his friend, Dr. Lanyon, and he notes that Dr. Lanyon seems to be on the verge of a complete physical collapse; Lanyon dies three weeks later. Among his papers is an envelope addressed to Utterson, and inside is an inner envelope, sealed with instructions that this envelope should not be opened until after Jekyll's death or disappearance. Utterson strongly feels that the contents of the envelope contain information about Edward Hyde.

On another Sunday walk, Utterson and Enfield pass along the street where Enfield saw Hyde trampling on the young girl. They step around the corner into the courtyard and see Dr. Jekyll in an upstairs window. Utterson invites Jekyll to accompany them on a walk, but suddenly Jekyll's face is covered with abject terror and, after a grimace of horrible pain, he suddenly closes the window and disappears. Utterson and Enfield are horrified by what they have seen.

Some time later, Utterson receives a visit from Poole, Dr. Jekyll's man servant. Poole suspects that foul play is associated with his employer; Dr. Jekyll, he says, has confined himself to his laboratory for over a week, has ordered all of his meals to be sent in, and has sent Poole on frantic searches to various chemists for a mysterious drug. Poole is now convinced that his employer has been murdered and that the murderer is still hiding in Jekyll's laboratory.

Utterson is sufficiently convinced that he returns to Jekyll's house, where he and Poole break into the laboratory. There, they discover that the mysterious figure in the laboratory has just committed suicide by drinking a vial of poison. The body is that of Edward Hyde. They search the entire building for signs of Jekyll and can find nothing, except a note addressed to Utterson.

The note informs Utterson that he should go home and read, first, the letter from Dr. Lanyon and then the enclosed document, which is the "confession" of Dr. Henry Jekyll.

Dr. Lanyon's narrative reveals that Dr. Jekyll had written to him, in the name of their old friendship, and had requested him to follow precise instructions: go to Jekyll's laboratory, secure certain items, bring them back to his house, and at twelve o'clock that night, a person whom Lanyon would not recognize would call for these things. Lanyon writes that he followed the instructions precisely and at exactly twelve o'clock, a horribly disagreeable, misbegotten "creature" appeared at the laboratory to claim the items for Dr. Jekyll. Before leaving, he asked for a "graduated glass," proceeded to mix the powders and liquids, and then drank the potion. To Dr. Lanyon's horror, the figure transformed before his eyes into that of Dr. Henry Jekyll. Lanyon closes his letter by pointing out that the man who stepped into the house that night to claim Jekyll's items was the man known as Edward Hyde.

The final chapter gives a fully detailed narration of Dr. Jekyll's double life. Jekyll had been born wealthy and had grown up handsome, honorable, and distinguished, and yet, he committed secret acts of which he was thoroughly ashamed; intellectually, he evaluted the differences between his private life and his public life and, ultimately, he became obsessed with the idea that at least two different entities, or perhaps even more, occupy a person's body. His reflections and his scientific knowledge led him to contemplate the possibility of scientifically isolating these two separate components. With this in mind, he began to experiment with various chemical combinations. Having ultimately compounded a certain mixture, he then drank it, and his body, under great pain, was transformed into an ugly, repugnant, repulsive "being," representing the "pure evil" that existed within him. Afterward, by drinking the same potion, he could then be transformed back into his original self.

His evil self became Edward Hyde, and in this disguise, he was able to practice whatever shameful depravities he wished, without feeling the shame that Dr. Jekyll would feel. Recognizing his two "selves," Jekyll felt the need of providing for, and protecting, Edward Hyde. Therefore, he furnished a house in Soho, hired a discreet and unscrupulous housekeeper, and announced to his servants that Mr. Hyde was to have full access and liberty of Jekyll's residence and, finally, he drew up a will leaving all of his inheritance to Edward Hyde. Thus, this double life continued until the murder of Sir Danvers Carew by Edward Hyde.

This horrible revelation caused Jekyll to make a serious attempt to cast off his evil side – that is, Edward Hyde – and for some time, he sought out the companionship of his old friends. However, the Edward Hyde side of his nature kept struggling to be recognized, and one sunny day while sitting in Regent's Park, he was suddenly transformed into Edward Hyde. It was at this time that he sought the help of his friend Dr. Lanyon. He hid in a hotel and wrote a letter asking Dr. Lanyon to go to the laboratory in his house and fetch certain drugs to Lanyon's house. There, Hyde drank the potion described in Lanyon's letter. The drug caused him to change to Dr. Jekyll, while Dr. Lanyon watched the transformation in utter horror.

After awhile, Edward Hyde almost totally occupied Jekyll's nature, and the original drug was no longer effective to return Hyde to Jekyll. After having Poole search throughout London for the necessary "powder," Jekyll realized that his original compound must have possessed some impurity which cannot now be duplicated. In despair at being forced to live the rest of his life as Hyde, he commits suicide at the moment that Utterson and Poole are breaking down the laboratory door.

LIST OF CHARACTERS

Mr. Gabriel John Utterson

The central character of the novel, who narrates most of the story, either directly or through documents which come into his possession. He is also the counsel for, and close friend to, both Dr. Jekyll and Dr. Lanyon.

Mr. Richard Enfield

A distant kinsman of Mr. Utterson, he is a well-known man about town and is the complete opposite of Mr. Utterson; yet they seem to thoroughly enjoy their weekly Sunday walks together.

Dr. Henry (Harry) Jekyll

A prominent physician in London; very handsome, distinguished, and generally respected; he has alienated some of his close professional friends because of his experiments concerning the dual nature of mankind.

Edward Hyde

As the name indicates, Hyde is the fleshy (or "sinful," according to Victorian standards) manifestation of Dr. Jekyll's personality; he is guilty of committing atrocious acts throughout the novel. The search to determine who Edward Hyde is constitutes the first half of the novel.

Dr. Hastie Lanyon

Dr. Jekyll's closest friend of many years; Lanyon broke with Jekyll concerning how much evil can be found within a person. Dr. Lanyon's narration in Chapter 9 reveals the true nature of Jekyll's and Hyde's relationship.

Poole

He is Dr. Jekyll's man servant, chief butler, and all-around manager of the house; he has been in Dr. Jekyll's service for so long that he knows every footstep and motion associated with his employer; he is, therefore, able to report to Mr. Utterson that the man in seclusion is not Dr. Jekyll.

Bradshaw

Dr. Jekyll's footman and man-about-the-house, who goes around to the back entry of Jekyll's laboratory to guard the back door, while Poole and Utterson break in through the front door.

Mr. Guest

Mr. Utterson's secretary, who is "a great student and critic of handwriting." He finds something amazingly similar between Dr. Jekyll's and Mr. Hyde's handwriting.

Sir Danvers Carew

A distinguished M.P. (Member of Parliament), who does not appear in the work, but whose unprovoked and vicious murder by Edward Hyde causes a turning point in the novel.

Inspector Newcomen of Scotland Yard

The officer who accompanies Utterson on a search of Hyde's house in Soho after the murder of Sir Danvers Carew.

SUMMARIES AND COMMENTARIES

CHAPTER 1

"Story of the Door"

When the novel opens, Mr. Utterson (a lawyer) and his friend Richard Enfield (a distant kinsman) are out for their customary Sunday stroll in London. People who know both men find it puzzling that the men are friends; seemingly, they have nothing in common. Yet both men look forward to their weekly Sunday walk as if it were "the chief jewel of each week." Mr. Utterson, the lawyer, is a cold man, very tall and lean, and has a face "never lighted by a smile." Enfield is much more outgoing and curious about life, and it is on this particular Sunday walk that he raises his cane and indicates a peculiar-looking door. He asks Utterson if he's ever noticed the door. With a slight change in his voice, Utterson says that he has, and then Enfield continues; the door, he tells Utterson, has "a very odd story."

Enfield says that at about 3 A.M. on a black winter morning, he was coming home and because the street was deserted, he had a vague sense of discomfort. Suddenly, he saw two figures, a man and a girl about eight years old. They ran into each other, and the man "trampled calmly over the child's body and left her screaming on the ground." He cannot forget the "hellish" scene.

He tells Utterson that he collared the man, brought him back, and by that time, a crowd had gathered. Like Enfield, they all seemed to instantly loathe the very sight of the sadistic man, who was, in contrast to the others, very calm and very cool. He said simply that he wanted to avoid a scene, and he offered to pay a generous sum to the child's family. Then he took out a key, opened the strange door, and disappeared behind it. He emerged shortly with ten pounds in gold and a check for ninety pounds. Enfield can't remember the precise signature on the check, but he does remember that it belonged to a well-known man. He tells his friend that he finds it extremely strange that this satanic man would just suddenly take out a key and open "the strange door," then walk out "with another man's check" for nearly one hundred pounds. Of course, Enfield says, he immediately thought that the check was forged, but the man agreed to wait until the banks opened, and when a teller was questioned, the check proved to be genuine. Enfield surmises that perhaps blackmail was involved, and ever since that winter morning, he has referred to that house as the "Black Mail House." He has "studied the place," and there seems to be no other door, and no one ever comes in or out, except, occasionally, the villainous man who ran down the child.

But Enfield feels strongly that someone else *must* live there, and yet the houses in that block are built so oddly and so compactly that he cannot ascertain where one house ends and the next house begins.

Utterson, the lawyer, tells his friend Enfield that sometimes it's best to mind one's own business, but he does want to know the name of the man who ran down the child. Enfield tells him that "it was a man of the name of Hyde." Asked to describe Hyde, Enfield finds it difficult because the man had "something wrong with his appearance, something displeasing, something downright detestable."

Utterson then asks a very lawyer-like question: "You are quite sure that he used a key?" He explains that he already knows the name of the other party involved in Enfield's story, and he wants Enfield to be as exact as possible. Enfield swears that everything he has said has been true: "The fellow had a key." And then he adds, "What's more, he has it still. I saw him use it, not a week ago."

Utterson sighs, and the two men make a pact never to speak of the horrible incident again, shaking hands to seal their agreement.

Commentary

The story of Dr. Jekyll and Mr. Hyde is perhaps one of the most familiar tales in all of literature. In fact, it is so familiar that many people assume that the tale has been in existence for longer than it actually has been. It is also familiar because the terminology (that is, the names of *Jekyll* and *Hyde*) is now a part of our common language and can be found in any dictionary. In fact, many people who have never heard of the name Robert Louis Stevenson can offer a reasonably acceptable meaning for the term "Jekyll and Hyde," and their explanation would not vary far from those found in selected or random dictionary definitions such as:

(1) "One who has quasi-schizophrenic, alternating phases of pleasantness and unpleasantness."
(2) "A person having a split personality, one side of which is good and the other evil."

(3) "This phrase refers to a person who alternates between charming demeanor and extremely unpleasant behavior."

In fact, the names of *Jekyll* and *Hyde* have even been used in
alcoholism manuals to describe the behavior of a sober person who
is kind and gentle but who unexpectedly changes into a vicious, cruel
person when drunk. The contrast in the behavior of a drunk and sober
person is therefore commonly referred to as the "Jekyll and Hyde
Syndrome."

All of the general views or above definitions of a "Jekyll and Hyde"
personality come almost entirely from the last two chapters of the
novel. Until then, the novel is presented as a closely knit mystery
story.

Another concept to keep in mind while reading this novel is that
the above definitions and all of the assumptions made about Jekyll
and Hyde are postulated on the assumption that man is made up of
only two parts – one good and one evil. This is not necessarily Stevenson's intent, as stated later by Dr. Jekyll, who thought that man's personality *might be* composed of many different facets, and that man's
evil nature was only a small portion of his total makeup. Consequently, when the transformation from Jekyll to Hyde occurs, Hyde cannot wear Jekyll's clothes because they are much too big for him –
that is, the evil part of Dr. Jekyll's total being, depicted through Hyde,
is represented as being much smaller than Jekyll. Thus, man is not
necessarily *equal* parts of good and evil; instead, the evil portion will
often express itself more forcefully and powerfully than do the other
aspects. However, for the sake of discussion, and since Dr. Jekyll himself admitted that he could detect only two sides of himself, we will
most often refer to Hyde as Jekyll's evil "double."

The entire nineteenth century was often concerned with the concept of man's double self, often referred to as a *Doppelgänger*, a term
taken from German literary criticism. This nineteenth-century genre
began with a story about a type of double, when Dr. Frankenstein
created his monster in 1818 (and due to popularizations of this story,
most people think that Frankenstein is the name of the monster instead of the scientist), and later, Sigmund Freud and others before
Stevenson wrote about man's contrasting natures – it was, however,
Stevenson's story of Jekyll and Hyde that has so completely held the

attention of readers throughout the decades. And as noted, the popularizations of a story will often distort parts of that story. For example, Stevenson intended the main character's name to be pronounced Je (the French word for "I") *Kill* (Je-*Kill* = I kill), meaning that the doctor wanted to isolate the evil portion of himself, appropriately named "Hyde," meaning low and vulgar hide or flesh which must *hide* from civilization. The character's name in the movies, however, was pronounced with the accent on the first syllable and it has remained so.

The *double* is also represented in even simpler ways in this novel. For example, Utterson and his kinsman, Richard Enfield, are so completely different from each other that people who know them are totally puzzled by their frequent walks together. Yet, as with the *double,* man is often drawn to someone totally opposite from himself.

Utterson, we discover, possesses those qualities that make him the perfectly reliable literary narrator. He is intellectual, objective, and tolerant; he is also reluctant to judge and is inclined to help people rather than to condemn them. And even though he is undemonstrative, he has won the deep trust of many important friends who confide in him and appoint him the executor of their estates. Consequently, Utterson makes the very best type of narrator since he is privy to the secrets of powerful men but is also discreet enough not to violate any trust.

In contrast, it is Enfield's vivacity, directness, and curiosity about life which involves us in the story as he narrates with gusto and enthusiasm his first horrible encounter with Edward Hyde. Thus, the reader's introduction to Hyde is through a "well-known man about town" who delights in entertaining people with strange and unusual stories. After this chapter, however, Enfield, as a narrator, is disposed of, and we will rely upon a more solid, restrained narrator such as Utterson.

The ultimate purpose of this novel (or tale) will be to demonstrate Dr. Jekyll's view of Hyde; yet this, as noted, is only the last portion of the novel. Before then, Stevenson will use several narrators and devices to present a number of opinions about Hyde. But, by using Enfield as the initial narrator, we get our first opinion about Hyde through Enfield, "the well-known man about town," and in describing his first encounter with Hyde, Enfield also gives us the views of all of the others gathered about when Hyde tramples the young girl underfoot. If we remember that Enfield is the type of person who prides himself on being a connoisseur of the beautiful, it might at first seem natural that he would over-exaggerate his own personal loathing for Hyde, especially since Enfield cannot specify any single deformity or any single distortion in Hyde's physique; rather, Enfield has simply a general sense of nausea and extreme distaste, so extreme that he senses that there is something unnatural about Hyde: "There was something wrong with his appearance; something displeasing, something downright detestable. I never saw a man I so disliked." But if we do not completely trust Enfield's sensibilities, then there are the reactions of the crowd of people which gathers at the scene and remains there to make sure that Hyde does not escape. For example, the women, upon looking at Hyde, suddenly seem to be "as wild as Harpies," and then the apothecary who is "as emotional as a bagpipe" turns sick upon seeing Hyde and has a strong desire to kill the man. Others, including the child's family, all possess this intense loathing for Hyde, accompanied with a desire to kill him.

This first chapter, then, presents not only Enfield's view of Hyde, but also the views of several others and, consequently, the reader is entranced about a person who can evoke such horrible responses in such differing types of people. And we should also note that Dr. Jekyll is not even mentioned – in fact, this part of London is built so strangely that it is not until quite some time later that we are able to discern that the particular door which evoked Enfield's narration is, in reality, the back door to Dr. Jekyll's laboratory. The novel begins, therefore, as a type of mystery story, in spite of the fact that there is probably no modern reader who can come to the novel without a previous knowledge that Hyde is really a part of Dr. Jekyll; but for the original audience, each of the subsequent chapters involved an attempt to discover the identity of Hyde and how he was blackmailing, or framing, or using Dr. Jekyll in some evil and probably obscene, horrible way.

CHAPTER 2

"Search for Mr. Hyde"

That evening, instead of coming home and ending the day with supper and "a volume of some dry divinity," Mr. Utterson (the lawyer) eats, and then he takes a candle and goes into his business room.

There, he opens a safe and takes out the will of Dr. Henry Jekyll. He ponders over it for a long time. The terms of the will stipulate that all of the doctor's possessions are "to pass into the hands of his friend and benefactor Edward Hyde" in case of – and this phrase, in particular, troubles Utterson – "Dr. Jekyll's 'disappearance or unexplained absence.'" Utterson realizes that, in essence, the will allows Edward Hyde to, in theory, "step into Dr. Jekyll's shoes . . . free from any burden or obligation." Utterson feels troubled and uneasy. The terms of the will offend his sense of propriety; he is "a lover of the sane and customary sides of life." Until now, Dr. Jekyll's will has seemed merely irregular and fanciful. Since Utterson's talk with Enfield, however, the name of Edward Hyde has taken on new and ominous connotations. Blowing out his candle, Utterson puts on his greatcoat and sets out for the home of a well-known London physician, Dr. Lanyon. Perhaps Lanyon can explain Dr. Jekyll's relationship to this fiendish Hyde person.

Dr. Lanyon is having a glass of wine when Utterson arrives, and he greets his old friend warmly; the two men have been close ever since they were in school and college together. They talk easily for awhile, and then Utterson remarks that Lanyon and he are probably "the two oldest friends that Henry Jekyll has." Lanyon replies that he himself hasn't seen much of Jekyll for ten years, ever since Jekyll "became too fanciful . . . wrong in mind." Utterson inquires about Edward Hyde, but Lanyon has never heard of the man. Thus, Utterson returns home, but he is uneasy; his dreams that night are more like nightmares, inhabited by Hyde's sense of evil and by a screaming, crushed child. Why, he frets, would Jekyll have such a man as Hyde as his beneficiary?

Utterson begins watching "the door" in the mornings, at noon, at night, and "at all hours of solitude." He must see this detestable man for himself. At last, Mr. Hyde appears. Utterson hears "odd, light footsteps drawing near," and when Hyde rounds the corner, Utterson steps up and, just as Hyde is inserting his key, Utterson asks, "Mr. Hyde, I think?"

Hyde shrinks back with a "hissing intake of breath." Then he collects his cool veneer: "That is my name. What do you want?" Utterson explains that he is an old friend of Dr. Jekyll's, and Hyde coldly tells him that Jekyll is away. Utterson asks to see Hyde's face clearly, and Hyde consents if Utterson will explain how he knew him. "We have common friends," Utterson says. Hyde is not convinced, and with a snarling, savage laugh, he accuses Utterson of lying. Then, with a sudden jerk, he unlocks the door and disappears inside.

The lawyer is stunned by Hyde's behavior. Enfield was right; Hyde *does* have a sense of "deformity . . . a sort of murderous mixture of timidity and boldness." Utterson realizes that until now he has never felt such loathing; the man seemed "hardly human." He fears for the life of his old friend Dr. Jekyll because he feels sure that he has read "Satan's signature on the face of Edward Hyde."

Sadly, Utterson goes around the corner and knocks at the second house in the block. The door is opened by Poole, Dr. Jekyll's elderly servant, who takes the lawyer in to wait by the fire. Utterson surveys the room, "the pleasantest room in London." But the face of Hyde poisons his thoughts, and he is suddenly filled with nausea and uneasiness. Poole returns and says that Jekyll is out. Utterson questions him about Hyde's having a key to "the old dissecting room." Poole replies that nothing is amiss: "Mr. Hyde has a key." Furthermore, he says, "we have all orders to obey him."

After Utterson leaves, he is stunned; he is absolutely convinced that his old friend Jekyll "is in deep waters"; perhaps the doctor is being haunted by "the ghost of some old sin, the cancer of some concealed disgrace." His thoughts return again to Mr. Hyde; he is positive that Hyde has "secrets of his own – black secrets." He must warn Jekyll; he feels that if Hyde knew the contents of Jekyll's will, he would not hesitate to murder the good doctor.

Commentary

At the end of Chapter 1, Stevenson suggests that Utterson knows more about Enfield's story than he is willing to admit. Remember that one of Utterson's qualities is his ability to keep strict confidences and remain always an honorable gentleman, even when indiscretion (such as opening Lanyon's letter prematurely) seems wise.

Now, in Chapter 2, we are given Utterson's own private narration, in which we discover that he is not only a close friend to Dr. Henry Jekyll, but he is also the executor of Jekyll's will. Thus, when Utterson returns once again to Jekyll's strange will and finds that *all* of his property under *any* circumstance is to be left to Edward Hyde, we now realize why Utterson was so fascinated with Enfield's narration.

In the first chapter, we were only distantly involved with Hyde. But now that we know that Hyde will be the sole inheritor of Dr. Jekyll's large estate, and as Utterson's fears increase, so do ours. In such a mystery story, the reader is expected to wonder about the possibility of Hyde's blackmailing Dr. Jekyll. Since we trust Utterson, who has a great fear for Jekyll, our own fears are also heightened.

When Utterson visits Hastie Lanyon, who was once Jekyll's closest friend (along with Utterson), and we hear that Lanyon has not seen Jekyll since Jekyll first advanced some very strange and "unscientific" theories, we then have our first hint that the mysterious Dr. Jekyll is involved in some sort of unacceptable or advanced medical practice – at least from the viewpoint of such a traditionalist as Lanyon. The exact nature of Jekyll's practice will not be revealed until the final chapter.

The most important scene in this chapter is Mr. Utterson's direct encounter with Edward Hyde. Note that even the staid Utterson will pun on Hyde's name: "If he be Mr. Hyde . . . I shall be Mr. Seek." And throughout the novel, the upright Mr. Utterson will seek to discover Mr. Hyde, who is the hidden, evil part of Dr. Jekyll. This chapter begins the search because it was only with great effort and great diligence (standing watch by "the door" day and night until Hyde finally appeared) and at a sacrifice of his other duties, that Utterson was able to talk with Hyde. This must show both an affection for Jekyll and a fear of Hyde.

Beginning with the previous chapter and at the end of this chapter, when Utterson is so deeply troubled, he begins to suspect Hyde of all sorts of things. And since Utterson speaks for the readers, we also begin to suspect Hyde of many things. Among the possibilities that Mr. Utterson entertains is the possibility that Hyde is blackmailing Jekyll. And before we know who Hyde really is, we suspect that he is doing all sorts of evil things: he might be a blackmailer, a forger, a potential murderer (and later, an actual murderer), a sadist, a man capable of committing any act of violence, a man of all sorts of unmentionable, unscrupulous conduct – in other words, a *thoroughly evil* man. In fact, Hyde is *all* of these, but what we never suspect is that he is also *a part of Dr. Jekyll.*

Mr. Utterson's opinion of Hyde conforms essentially to Enfield's view of Hyde. Utterson also sees him as "dwarfish," and he says that Hyde "gave an impression of deformity without any nameable malformation." For some unexplained reason, Utterson regards Hyde with a "hitherto unknown disgust, loathing, and fear." It is as though he is able "to read Satan's signature upon a face." Later that night, the *thought* of Hyde causes a "nausea and distaste of life."

If we now examine the actions of Hyde, we will see that in the first chapter, he knocked a girl down without any twinge of guilt. He made no deliberate attempt to harm the girl – there was no deliberate maliciousness or cruelty. Stevenson uses the phrase "like a Juggernaut," a word which suggests that Hyde's action was one of complete indifference – not an evil-conceived, satanic act. In fact, Hyde stood by and took (or assumed) complete responsibility for his actions and made recompense fully commensurate with his cruel act.

Yet, however, his very presence and appearance arouse a sense of absolute evil in the beholder. In other words, Hyde is the type of person who evokes the worst in the beholder and causes the beholder to want to commit some type of horrible crime – even murder. Stevenson seems to be saying that Hyde is a part of *all* people, and the very sight of Hyde brings out the worst in us; therefore, we want to kill and reject that evil part of our nature, as Dr. Jekyll will attempt to do. As we will see later, the mere sight of Hyde and the realization of the evil he represents will kill Lanyon, and we must assume that before Utterson knows who Hyde really is, that the man has the most disturbing effect on Utterson's life of anything he has ever encountered. And remember that the first chapter announced that Utterson was one who was given to tolerance; he was a person slow to judge other people for their vices. But just as Jekyll will find out that he cannot reject a part of himself, Stevenson seems to suggest that his readers, while being repulsed by Hyde, can never fully reject the Hyde aspect of their natures.

CHAPTER 3

"Dr. Jekyll was Quite at Ease"

Two weeks later, Dr. Jekyll gives a small dinner party, for which, we gather, he is well known, for the narrator refers to it as being "one of his pleasant dinners." Five or six of Dr. Jekyll's old cronies are invited, and among them is Mr. Utterson. As usual, the food is superb, the wine good, and Utterson manages to be the last guest to leave.

Utterson has often been one of the last guests to leave Jekyll's dinner parties, so Jekyll thinks nothing of Utterson's lingering behind. In fact, Jekyll is pleased, for he likes Utterson very much. Often, after his guests have departed, he and Utterson have sat and talked together, quietly relaxing after the noisy chatter of the dinner party.

Tonight, as they sit beside a crackling fire, Jekyll, a large man of perhaps fifty, warmly smiles at Utterson, and the lawyer answers Jekyll's smile with a question. He asks Jekyll about his will.

At this point, the narrator speaks to us directly; he says that "a close observer" might have detected that the topic was "distasteful" to Jekyll, but that Jekyll very carefully controlled his reactions to Utterson's question. Assuming a feigned, light-hearted and rather condescending tone, Jekyll chides Utterson for being so concerned about the will. He compares Utterson's anxiety to Dr. Lanyon's "hide-bound" stuffiness. Now, we realize that Dr. Lanyon did not reveal to Utterson his real reason for being so disappointed in Jekyll. Jekyll, however, unknowingly reveals more to us – and to Utterson – about Dr. Lanyon's distaste for Jekyll's scientific interests, interests which Dr. Lanyon told Jekyll were "scientific heresies."

Jekyll says that he still likes Lanyon, but that as a scientist, Dr. Lanyon is limited – too old-fashioned and conservative, too much of a "hide-bound pedant." Then Jekyll becomes more emotional. Dr. Lanyon, he says, is "an ignorant, blatant pedant. I was never more disappointed in any man than Lanyon."

Utterson, however, is firm about the subject at hand. He returns to the original subject of Dr. Jekyll's will. He says again that he strongly disapproves of the terms of Jekyll's will. In answer, Jekyll says that he knows that Utterson disapproves of the will. Utterson will not drop the subject. He tells Jekyll that he disapproves of the will more strongly now than ever because of some new information that he has concerning Edward Hyde.

When Jekyll hears the name of Hyde, the narrator tells us, "the large, handsome face of Dr. Jekyll" grows pale. Jekyll says that he wants to hear no more. But Utterson insists: "What I heard was abominable."

Jekyll becomes confused; he stammers. Concerning Hyde, Jekyll says that Utterson will never understand. His relationship with Hyde is "painful . . . a very strange one." Jekyll says that his relationship with Hyde is "one of those affairs that cannot be mended by talking."

Utterson pleads with his old friend to "make a clean breast"; he will keep everything confidential. He promises that, if he can, he will get Jekyll out of this "painful relationship." But Jekyll's mind is resolute. He says that he knows Utterson means well, and that of all his friends, he would trust Utterson to help him most, but that "it is not so bad as that." He says that he can, at any moment he chooses, "be rid of Hyde." He profusely thanks Utterson for his concern, and then asks him to look on the subject as a private matter and "let it sleep."

Utterson is silent; he gazes into the fire, then gets to his feet. Jekyll says that he hopes that the two of them will never talk about "poor Hyde" again. He says that he has "a very great interest in Hyde," and that if he is "taken away," he wants Utterson to promise him that Hyde will get everything entitled to him in Jekyll's will.

Utterson is blunt; he is sure that he can *never* like Hyde. Jekyll says that he doesn't ask Utterson to *like* Hyde; he merely asks Utterson to promise that he will give Hyde, as beneficiary, all of Jekyll's estate: "I only ask for justice . . . when I am no longer here." Heaving a sigh, Utterson agrees: "I promise."

Commentary

This chapter presents another side of Utterson; for example, we discover that "where Utterson was liked, he was well liked. Hosts loved to detain the dry lawyer." This quality in Utterson, therefore, allows him to linger after Jekyll's party so as to be able to discuss Jekyll's will with him.

And thus, for the first time in the novel, we meet the other character in the novel's title. And the most immediately noticeable thing about him is that he is an extremely handsome man. This, of course, contrasts with the other part of himself – that is, Hyde, who is extremely loathsome. Also, Jekyll is a well proportioned, large man, as contrasted to the dwarfish Hyde. Symbolically, then, Hyde, the evil part of Dr. Jekyll, represents only a small portion of the total makeup of Dr. Jekyll. Also, Hyde is much younger than Jekyll, suggesting that the evil portion of Jekyll has not existed as long as has the "total" Dr. Jekyll, and later in Jekyll's "confession," he does speak of his youthful indiscretions, which occurred probably in, or around, his twenties.

The contrast between Dr. Jekyll and Dr. Lanyon was presented in the last chapter by Dr. Lanyon, who thought that Jekyll was "too fanciful" or too metaphysical, and he, therefore, rejected Dr. Jekyll's theories. Now we see that Dr. Jekyll views Lanyon as a "hidebound pedant" who is too distressed to investigate new and startling concepts. Ultimately, Dr. Jekyll refers to Lanyon as "an ignorant, blatant pedant."

When the two men discuss Dr. Jekyll's will, Utterson feels a professional obligation to advise his friend to change his will. In fact, Utterson tries to get Jekyll to confess what horrible sin or crime aligns him with this "abominable" Mr. Hyde: "Make a clean breast of this in confidence; and I make no doubt I can get you out of it." When Utterson confesses that he can never "like" this abominable man, Jekyll is also aware of this: "I don't ask that . . . I only ask for justice; I only ask you to help him for my sake, when I am no longer here." The irony, of course, is that while Utterson is so adamantly opposed to Hyde, he does not know that he is attacking a part of Jekyll to Jekyll's face.

This chapter occurs early in the Jekyll/Hyde relationship, and Jekyll is able to assure Utterson that "the moment I choose, I can be rid of Mr. Hyde. I give you my hand upon that." But it is Jekyll's choice to keep Hyde around—for awhile. Originally, the ultimate aim of Dr. Jekyll's experiment was to discover his evil nature and isolate or reject it. But he became fascinated with this evil side of his nature. And as we will later see, Jekyll will reach a point where he can't control Hyde, who will begin to appear unexpectedly and begin to rule Jekyll's life.

CHAPTER 4

"The Carew Murder Case"

This chapter begins almost a year later and recounts the details of the murder of Sir Danvers Carew, a well-known and highly respected London gentleman. Carew was murdered near midnight on a foggy, full-moon night in October, and his murder was witnessed by a maid who worked and lived in a house not far from the Thames. That night, she went upstairs to bed about eleven o'clock and, because the night was so mysteriously romantic, she sat gazing out of her bedroom window for a time, "in a dream of musing." Never, she tells the police, had she felt happier and more at peace with the world.

Ironically, her mood of languid revery is broken, for as she gazes down beneath her window, she recognizes the "small" figure of Mr. Hyde, a man who had once visited her master and for whom she had *immediately* taken an instant dislike. From her window that October night, the woman saw the detestable Mr. Hyde meet "an aged and beautiful gentleman with white hair"; then suddenly, after a few words, Mr. Hyde lifted his heavy walking stick and clubbed the old gentleman to death. Indeed, the blows which he struck were so thunderous that "bones were audibly shattered," and then, "with ape-like fury," Hyde trampled the old gentleman underfoot. At the horror of what she saw, the maid suddenly fainted.

When the police arrive on the scene, they find no identification on the body, and they are puzzled that neither the victim's gold watch nor his wallet was taken. The only bit of evidence they discover concerning the man's identity is a sealed envelope addressed to Mr. Utterson. Thus, they call Utterson, and he is able to identify the corpse. The police are visibly stunned. "This will make a deal of noise," they comment, meaning that the case will draw a lot of publicity because Sir Danvers was such a well-known figure in London society and politics.

When Utterson is shown the murder weapon, he recognizes it immediately. It is the battered half of a walking cane which he gave Dr. Jekyll many years ago. He reflects for a moment and then tells the police officer to come with him; he can lead them to the murderer's quarters.

On the way to Hyde's apartment, the narrator describes in much detail the "chocolate-colored wreaths" of fog that they drive through on their way to "the dismal quarter" where Hyde lives. This district, says the narrator, seems "like a district of some city in a nightmare." Yet this is where Edward Hyde, heir to Jekyll's quarter of a million pounds, lives.

The woman who answers their knock tells them that Hyde is not at home; in fact, last night was the first night that he had been home in nearly two months; "his habits were very irregular." When Utterson introduces the officer as being from Scotland Yard, he is sure that the old silver-haired woman seems almost to relish the prospect of Hyde's being in trouble. They search Hyde's apartment and immediately see that Hyde left in a hurry. Clothes are thrown here and there, drawers are pulled out, and on the hearth is a pile of grey ashes.

The inspector stirs the embers and finds half of a checkbook. Behind a door, he also discovers the other half of the murder weapon, the heavy walking stick.

Delighted with what he has found, the inspector and Utterson visit Hyde's bank and ascertain that Hyde's account contains several thousand pounds. The officer is sure that Hyde can be captured now because "money's life to the man." All he has to do now, he says, is post handbills with Hyde's picture and a description of the man. However, this proves to be an almost impossible task because Hyde has no family, and seemingly, he was never photographed. Moreover, of those who have seen him, no one has seen him more than two times. The only thing that everyone agrees on is that Hyde carries "a haunting sense of unexpressed deformity."

Commentary

Since a year has elapsed since the last chapter, we can never know what Hyde has been doing, what atrocities he has committed and what degradations he has stooped to. Apparently, they have been many and numerous because he has moved from being a creature who tramples on a child in the first chapter to this chapter, where he commits an unprovoked murder. In other words, Hyde's capacity for evil is increasing.

The crime, a murder of a distinguished, well-known social and political figure, is committed by the light of the full moon. Here, Stevenson is using the full moon so that from a practical point-of-view, the upstairs maid can clearly see and describe the encounter between Hyde and Sir Danvers, but also, the full moon, in terms of superstition, is the time when evil beings, often in the shape of deformed men or werewolves, commit their most heinous acts.

The crime seems to be without motivation. Yet Stevenson is careful to describe Hyde's reaction to Sir Danvers. Sir Danvers is described as "an aged and beautiful gentleman with white hair." He also seemed to "breathe . . . an innocent and old-world kindness of disposition"; in addition, he was also noble and high-minded. If, therefore, Hyde represents pure evil, he would naturally detest meeting such a "good" gentleman, one who is the direct opposite of Hyde's loathsome self. And in murdering the innocent and noble Sir Danvers, Hyde is described as having an "ape-like fury," one who is maddened with rage to the point of committing the most unspeakable horror against innocence. It is as though Hyde was not content to simply murder the distinguished man – he had to completely destroy him; he even mangled the dead body so that the bones were audibly shattered and even then, he was not yet content – he had to trample upon his victim. It is as though the goodness of Sir Danvers brings out the most intense evil in Hyde.

Utterson is unexpectedly drawn into the case since Sir Danvers was another of his distinguished clients, again suggesting the ultimate importance and influence of Utterson. This seeming coincidence then allows Utterson to be in on the investigation of Sir Danvers' death and to report accurately all of the findings.

When the body is definitely identified as being that of Sir Danvers, Inspector Newcomen of Scotland Yard is immediately appalled, suggesting, therefore, the public fame connected with the murdered man. Thus, this is not just a murder, but the murder of a renowned man of government, and his murder affects the entire nation more than would, say, the murder of a common citizen; the murder of a high public official directly interferes with the smooth and safe operation of the government.

When Utterson takes the inspector to Hyde's address, he, of course, takes him to the address in Soho, not to Dr. Jekyll's "back door." There, they are met by Hyde's housekeeper, a woman with an "evil face, smoothed by hypocrisy." This type of housekeeper would be appropriate for Hyde since she would be closed-mouthed about Hyde's evil doings, but even this evil housekeeper seems to take delight in the fact that Hyde has gotten into trouble. Again, apparently Hyde's propensity for evil has increased over the past year.

When the inspector has the murderer identified and discovers that the murderer has several thousands of pounds (in today's monetary spending capacity, this would be more than fifty thousand dollars), he is sure that he will be able to apprehend the criminal. Yet, as he wants to prepare a description of Hyde and publish a photo of him, he can find only a few people who can describe him, but no photograph of Hyde exists. It is as though Hyde doesn't exist – as indeed he *doesn't*, except in terms of Dr. Jekyll.

CHAPTER 5

"Incident of the Letter"

Mr. Utterson goes immediately to Dr. Jekyll's residence and is admitted by Poole, who takes him out of the house and across a former garden to the "dissecting rooms." They enter, climb a flight of stairs, enter a door covered with imitation red felt and, at last, Utterson sees Dr. Jekyll, "looking deadly sick." He is alone and sitting beside a fireplace in a dim, dusty-windowed room. Utterson asks him if he has heard the news about Sir Danvers. Jekyll says that he heard the paperboys yelling about it earlier. Utterson is firm. He asks only one question of the doctor: surely his old friend has not been "mad enough" to have hidden Hyde. Jekyll assures Utterson that he will never again set eyes on Hyde, that Hyde is "quite safe," and that he will never be heard of again. Utterson is concerned, however, and betrays his anxiety for his old friend Jekyll. At this, Jekyll takes out a note and asks Utterson to study it and keep it for him. Utterson opens the note. It is from Hyde, assuring Jekyll that he should not worry about Hyde's safety, for he, Hyde, has a sure means of escape. Utterson asks Jekyll bluntly if Hyde dictated the terms of Jekyll's will, particularly the clause that contains the words, "the possibility of Jekyll's disappearance." When Jekyll is seized with "a qualm of faintness," Utterson's mouth grows tight. He was sure of Hyde's part in making the terms of the doctor's will. He asks Jekyll if there was an envelope for the note, and the doctor tells him that there was, but that he burned the envelope. It bore no postmark, however. Utterson tells the doctor that he has had a narrow escape, for Hyde obviously meant to murder the doctor. Jekyll covers his face with his hands, moaning about the horrible lesson he has learned.

As Utterson is leaving, he questions Poole about the note that Jekyll gave him: what sort of messenger delivered it? Poole tells the lawyer that there has been no messenger. Furthermore, nothing came in the mail except some circulars. This news alarms Utterson. Clearly, the note came from Hyde. Thus, Hyde must have given it to Jekyll in the dissecting rooms.

Utterson leaves amidst the shouting of newsboys, still hawking papers about the murder of Sir Danvers. When he is at last at home, alone except for his head clerk, Mr. Guest, Utterson sits pondering the details of the case. And then, "insensibly," according to the narrator, the lawyer asks Guest, who happens to be a "great student and critic of handwriting," if he will study the note which Jekyll gave him and if he will comment on it. As the clerk is studying the note, he comments that the man who wrote it is "not mad" (earlier, Guest had commented that Sir Danvers' murderer was certainly mad), but that the note is written in "an odd hand." Just then, a servant enters, carrying an invitation from Jekyll to Utterson, asking the lawyer to dinner. Guest asks Utterson if he may see the invitation and compare the handwriting to the handwriting on the note.

After a pause, Utterson asks why Guest is comparing the two specimens of handwriting. Guest tells him that "there's a rather singular resemblance; the two hands are in many points identical; only differently sloped."

When Utterson is alone, he locks the note in his safe. He is horrified. Henry Jekyll, he is sure, forged the note that was supposedly written by Edward Hyde, the murderer of Sir Danvers. His old friend, the doctor, forged a note to cover up for a murderer!

Commentary

At the beginning of this chapter, when Utterson goes to visit Dr. Jekyll, he is admitted to Jekyll's laboratory for the first time. In fact, he was not even aware of the existence of this part of the property (and the three "dusty windows barred with iron" will later be the windows where Utterson and Enfield will see Dr. Jekyll sitting, in Chapter 7). Note that when Utterson meets Dr. Jekyll here, he is aware that an immense change has taken place in the doctor: Dr. Jekyll looked "deadly sick." He did not rise to meet his visitor, but held out a cold hand and "bade him welcome in a changed voice." Dr. Jekyll's sickness, of course, symbolically represents his sick conscience that is shocked that such a horrible murder could take place, for he, of course, knows that he (or a part of him) is responsible for the crime.

It is likewise ironic that when Utterson asks Jekyll directly, "You have not been mad enough to *hide* this fellow," the pun on *hide* is challenging, because the reason for the creation of Hyde was so that Dr. Jekyll could indeed hide his own debaucheries behind Hyde and still live his own respectable life as Dr. Jekyll. And when the doctor assures Utterson that "I swear to God I will never set eyes on him again. I bind my honor to you that I am done with him in this world," we assume (along with Utterson) that Dr. Jekyll is speaking the truth; however, this is an oath that will be impossible to keep because Hyde has too much of a grasp on Dr. Jekyll, who will indeed, as in the next chapter, hide Hyde for awhile, but eventually Hyde will emerge on his own terms.

When Utterson again points out to Dr. Jekyll the possibility that he and his name would be dragged through a trial if Hyde is ever caught, Dr. Jekyll again insists that "I am quite done with him." Again, the point is that since his early youth, Dr. Jekyll has tried to outwardly live an exemplary life, and his creation of Hyde was done out of scientific curiosity and also so that Dr. Jekyll could participate in debaucheries without danger of detection; therefore, now, the fear of scandal makes the doctor resolve to never see Hyde again. As Dr. Jekyll says, "I was thinking of my own character, which this hateful business has rather exposed." And too, he has always feared that his distinguished reputation would be stained by his secret, dubious activities.

We should also note that when Dr. Jekyll's servant, Poole, assures Utterson that no letter was delivered by a messenger, we assume along with Utterson that Hyde *must* have delivered it by the laboratory door – the door which Enfield had observed in Chapter 1. It is, after all, fitting that such a person as Hyde would use only the *back* door.

While Utterson functions as the central intelligence of the first part of the novel, we should always be aware that much of the information by which we formulate our opinions concerning Jekyll/Hyde come from different sources. For example, written documents, such as Dr. Jekyll's will, tell us a great deal, but we also rely upon Utterson to theorize about it. And we should also note that Utterson's theories or conjectures will always be *wrong* – because his knowledge does not include the workings of an actual separation of a Jekyll/Hyde phenomenon. For example, in this chapter, after the murder, he will confront Dr. Jekyll and ask him directly if it wasn't Hyde who forced him to make certain concessions in the will. Dr. Jekyll admits (by a nod) that it was. This, of course, is misleading, but – at this point – we accept Utterson's analysis. Likewise in this chapter, we have another document – the letter in which Hyde writes that he is disappearing forever. Again, we are misled when Utterson's trusted, confidential clerk, an expert on handwriting, reads the letter and offers the proposition that both Hyde's letter and the invitation which Utterson has just received from Dr. Jekyll were written by the same person, only with a slightly different slope in the handwriting. Immediately, Utterson is alarmed, thinking that once again, Dr. Jekyll has forged the letter to cover up for the evil Mr. Hyde. And again, we accept Utterson's theory, but what is ironic is the fact that since Dr. Jekyll and Mr. Hyde are one person, Utterson is, of course, right, but in a way that neither the reader nor Utterson could ever suspect.

CHAPTER 6

"Remarkable Incident of Doctor Lanyon"

Despite the fact that thousands of pounds are offered for Sir Danvers' murderer, Scotland Yard receives no information. Seemingly, Hyde has vanished. Yet, if the man himself has disappeared, past stories about him continue to surface. More tales about his past acts of cruelty are uncovered, and a general sense of Hyde's vile and violent life remains. But, as for the man Hyde, it is as though Jekyll was right: Hyde seems to have permanently left his quarters in Soho (then, a down-and-out, bohemian section of London) and escaped – never to be heard of again.

Coincidentally, just as the disappearance of Hyde seems to be a matter of fact, Jekyll's sanity and his sense of good health return. The doctor comes out of his self-imposed seclusion and begins giving dinner parties again. He is seen often in public, and people take note of how happy and healthy he looks. For two months, it seems as though Dr. Jekyll immensely enjoys life once more.

Yet, on January 8, Utterson dined with Jekyll, and only four days after this festive and merry dinner party, Utterson goes to see his old friend and is turned away by Poole. Likewise, he is turned away several more times. Utterson becomes concerned. He had come to believe that both Jekyll's mental and physical health had returned to him. But now it seems that Jekyll has lapsed into a grave illness that threatens both his body and his soul. For that reason, Utterson hurries off to see Dr. Lanyon.

He is relieved to find that the doctor is at home, but when he sees Lanyon, he is stunned to discover that his old friend is terribly ill. Lanyon "had his death-warrant written legibly upon his face."

Utterson senses that Lanyon, however, is not dying of physical decay; it seems as though he is a victim of some "deep-seated terror" within his mind. Utterson cannot help himself; he remarks on how very ill Lanyon looks, and the doctor admits that indeed, he is seriously ill. "I have had a shock," he tells Utterson, and when Utterson mentions their friend Jekyll's similar illness, Lanyon's face changes. He says that he never wishes to see or talk about Dr. Jekyll. He is vehement: he is done with the doctor; from now on, he will regard Jekyll as being already dead.

Utterson protests at such a display of hatred, but Lanyon is firm. He never wants to see Jekyll again. He tells Utterson that perhaps someday Utterson will learn about the "right and wrong of this." The phrase "of this" eludes Utterson; he cannot fathom what Lanyon is referring to, but whatever "this" may be, it is sufficient to cause Lanyon to tell Utterson that if he cannot talk about a subject other than Jekyll, he must leave.

When Utterson returns home, he sits down and writes a letter to Jekyll, asking straightforwardly for an answer about why he and Lanyon have quarreled. The following day, he receives Jekyll's answer. But after reading the doctor's letter, Utterson knows no more than he did formerly.

Jekyll shares Lanyon's view that the two old friends must never meet again. As for himself, Jekyll says that he intends to lead a very secluded life from now on. However, he pleads with Utterson to believe in Jekyll's genuine friendship for him, but he asks Utterson to trust him to know what is best for all concerned. "I have to go my own dark way," Jekyll says, and it is a way that Utterson must not try and follow. He says further that he has brought a terrible punishment and a danger on himself; he never imagined that he could, or would, become "the chief of sinners," or that the earth contained such "sufferings and terrors"; he begs Utterson to respect his fervent wish for absolute privacy and solitude.

The lawyer's worst fears are confirmed. The old "dark influence" has returned and enveloped Jekyll; only a few weeks ago, it seemed impossible – Jekyll had seemed to be healthy and cheerful. Now, all that has changed, and what is more, Jekyll has condemned himself to a living hell. Utterson is tempted to diagnose the malady as simply madness, but because of Lanyon's frenzied condemnation of Dr. Jekyll and because of his ambiguity about his reasons for hating Jekyll so thoroughly, surely it is more than simple madness which now consumes Jekyll. There must be something else.

Less than three weeks later, Lanyon is dead. After the funeral, Utterson returns home and goes to his business office; there, by candlelight, he takes out a sealed envelope and studies it. Written on the outside of the envelope is: "PRIVATE: for the hands of G. J. Utterson Alone, and in case of his predecease to be *destroyed unread.*" The emphasis on these last two words puzzles Utterson. Reluctantly, he decides to open the envelope. Within, there is another envelope, also sealed, with instructions "*not* to be opened till the death or disappearance of Dr. Henry Jekyll."

Utterson's mind reels; the same phrase that he read in Jekyll's will, "death or disappearance," confronts him anew, flooding him with black, sinister waves of revulsion for Edward Hyde. Without a doubt, Lanyon's writing is on both envelopes, and thus the mystery concerning Hyde, Jekyll, and Lanyon mounts, and as much as Utterson longs to solve the mystery once and for all, he cannot betray his old friend's honor and faith. Thus, he replaces the inner envelope into the outer envelope and replaces both of them in his safe once again. Then he goes to Jekyll's apartment, but Poole has unpleasant news. The doctor, he says, lives almost continually alone in the single, small room over the laboratory; he does not read, and he says very little. Something terrible seems to be preying on his mind.

Utterson continues to return to Jekyll's quarters, but each time, Poole has the same melancholy news: Jekyll is living alone above the laboratory and seeing no one. Thus, Utterson's futile visits become fewer and fewer.

Commentary

At the opening of the chapter, when the police are investigating Hyde's life and deeds, and we hear about the numerous vile practices he has committed, we now realize that during the year that elapses between Chapters 3 and 4, Hyde had apparently practiced every type of vile and violent deed and "had collected a multitude of enemies." This causes Utterson to utter "the death of Sir Danvers was . . . more than paid for by the disappearance of Mr. Hyde." This is not a callous statement when we realize the extreme extent of the evil practiced by Hyde. Utterson is the type who would gladly sacrifice a single life if it insured the riddance of a universal evil which Hyde now appears to be.

It is also symbolic that once Dr. Jekyll has rejected Hyde, Jekyll changes completely. In medical terms, he has purged himself of some deep disease that was eating away at him. With Hyde gone, for some time (Sir Danvers was murdered by Hyde in October, and it is now early January), Jekyll has changed back into his old social self and has been a delightful host. Thus, it is even more puzzling when Jekyll suddenly reverts to his old secretive self. The explanation for this episode is not given until Chapter 10, when Jekyll explains that he was sitting in Regent's Park, when suddenly, to his horror, he became Edward Hyde and found himself clad in the over-sized clothes of Dr. Jekyll. The shock of this transformation occurring without the use of his potion causes the doctor to totally isolate himself.

During Utterson's visit to Dr. Lanyon, he discovers the man to be the victim of some unknown terror which has literally announced his doom – he will be dead in three weeks. What Utterson or the reader does not know is that by the chronological time of Utterson's conversation with Lanyon, Dr. Lanyon has already been exposed to the events narrated in his document that we will read in Chapter 9. That is, on the 8th of January, Utterson had dined with Dr. Jekyll and yet it is only two days later when Lanyon received the letter from Jekyll, dated January 10th, begging for help, and it was then that Lanyon was exposed to the fact that Jekyll and Hyde are the same. We do not know this until later, but the novel is already looking forward to that knowledge, and we can now understand Dr. Lanyon's total collapse.

The cause of Lanyon's death – the horror – is not fully clear until the entire novel is considered. It must be remembered that both men had once been very close friends and that both men are eminent in their professions. Likewise, we ultimately know that Dr. Lanyon has disapproved of Dr. Jekyll on professional grounds – that Jekyll's *metaphysical* speculations about human behavior transcend the true limits of physical medicine, that Dr. Jekyll's ideas are "too fanciful" for him, and thus they broke company. However, no matter how metaphysical or fanciful Dr. Jekyll's *ideas* are, when Dr. Lanyon was exposed to the *reality* of the speculations in the person of Hyde, who before Lanyon's eyes became Jekyll, it horrifies him. The actual horror of the discovery that Jekyll and Hyde are one person lies *not* in the discovery itself, but in the full realization concerning the nature of evil in *all* *men*. The effect of Lanyon's being exposed directly to EVIL INCARNATE is simply too monstrous for Dr. Lanyon to absorb, admit, or handle because this would mean that every person, including Dr. Lanyon, is partly evil. The shock of this realization therefore kills him. A similar type of idea is found earlier in the century in Nathaniel Hawthorne's story "Young Goodman Brown"; Brown went forth into the forest, where he had a vision of evil, in which he saw all of the good ministers and goodwomen and even his wife, Faith, in secret conspiracy with the Devil. After that night, Young Goodman Brown was forever a changed and gloomy man. A direct confrontation with the personification of evil in the person of Edward Hyde and his transformation back into Jekyll was simply more than the good Dr. Lanyon could handle.

Utterson's character is put to a test in this chapter. Upon Dr. Lanyon's death and the receipt of the envelope with the instructions "not to be opened till the death or disappearance of Dr. Henry Jekyll," Utterson is sore put *not* to obey his friend's request.

Having lost one friend, Dr. Lanyon, and fearing the loss of Dr. Jekyll because of the strange wording "death or disappearance" – the same words Jekyll used in his will – all of these things combine to tempt Utterson to violate Lanyon's trust and open the envelope, especially since it might contain some information which might help save Dr. Jekyll. But "professional honor and faith to his dead friend" restrain him from opening the envelope, which he locks away in his safe.

CHAPTER 7

"Incident at the Window"

Mr. Utterson and Mr. Enfield are taking one of their customary Sunday strolls and, by chance, their path takes them past "that door," the door that they agreed never to speak of again. They pause now and look at it. Enfield thinks that Mr. Hyde will never be heard of again, and Utterson is quick to agree. He then asks Enfield if he ever told his old friend that he actually saw Hyde, and, furthermore, that when he saw the man, he was filled with a fierce feeling of revulsion. Enfield remarks that it's impossible to see Hyde and not feel nauseated.

Utterson suggests that they step into the courtyard for a look at the windows, and as they do, he reveals his uneasiness about Dr. Jekyll's health. Ominously, he says that perhaps just "the presence of a friend" outside, in the court, might strengthen the poor man.

The two men survey the windows of Jekyll's quarters, and their eyes are drawn to one window in particular. It is half-open and sitting close beside it, looking like a prisoner in solitary confinement, is Dr. Jekyll. Unhesitatingly, Utterson calls out to the doctor, "Jekyll, I trust you are better."

Jekyll's reply is dreary: he feels low, very low, and fears that he "will not last long, thank God." Trying to cheer his old friend, Utterson urges Jekyll to get out – "whip up the circulation" – and he invites Jekyll to join him and Enfield.

Jekyll sighs. He says that Utterson is a good man for suggesting a stroll together, but he cannot join them; he dare not. Yet, he stresses that he is very glad to see Utterson, and he would like to invite the two men up, but "the place is really not fit." Utterson suggests then that they converse where they are, and the suggestion causes Jekyll to turn and smile at them. But suddenly his features convulse and freeze in an expression of "abject terror and despair." The narrator tells us that the change in Jekyll's expression was so instantaneous and so horrible that it "froze the very blood of the two gentlemen below."

Jekyll's window is jerked down so viciously that, without a word, Utterson and Enfield turn and leave the courtyard. They do not speak to one another until they reach a neighboring thoroughfare, where there are "still some stirrings of life." Both men are so pale that when they look at one another, there is "an answering horror in their eyes."

Utterson speaks softly, "God forgive us, God forgive us." Enfield nods, and the two men walk on once more in silence.

Commentary

Chapter 7 is obviously the shortest chapter in the novel, only about two pages long, but it contains a key scene: during the walk that Utterson and Enfield take, they find themselves before that same door which prompted Enfield to relate the story of his encounter with Hyde in Chapter 1. Likewise, here are the three windows that were half-open in Jekyll's laboratory, described in Chapter 5. Now the reader

36

is fully aware of the significance of the *front* of Jekyll's house with its great facade and its elegant interior, as contrasted to the *back* entrance (Hyde's entrance), with its dilapidated structure.

Some readers and students feel cheated that Stevenson does not fully reveal what Utterson saw at the window in Jekyll's face just before Jekyll slams the window down and disappears. We must only assume that suddenly Jekyll takes on some of Hyde's traits, and that now both Utterson and Enfield have had a glimpse of the duality of man, of the evil that resides in the soul of man. But whereas Lanyon was a man who could not tolerate such an insight, Utterson and Enfield both belong to a different world. Enfield is "that man about town" who has theoretically seen many sorts of things, and Utterson, from the first pages, is a man who is not quick to judge his fellow man. Yet each of these men, upon seeing something in Dr. Jekyll's face, feel "abject terror and despair" and what they see freezes "the very blood of the two gentlemen."

CHAPTER 8

"The Last Night"

One evening after dinner, Utterson is sitting peacefully beside his fireplace when he receives a visit by a very agitated and upset Mr. Poole. He offers Poole a glass of wine to calm him, and although Poole accepts it, he neglects to drink it as he hesitatingly tells Utterson about his fears concerning Dr. Jekyll. Poole is terribly afraid. He fears that there has been "foul play," the nature of which he "daren't say." At this, Utterson grabs up his hat and his greatcoat, and the two men set forth in the wild, cold March night for Jekyll's house. When they arrive at Jekyll's quarters, a servant opens the door very guardedly, asking, "Is that you, Poole?" Once inside, Utterson finds all of Jekyll's servants "huddled together like a flock of sheep," and when they see Utterson, one maid breaks into "hysterical whimpering." This matter is far more serious than Utterson ever imagined. Several of the servants try to speak up, but Poole silences them and leads Utterson through the back garden, warning the lawyer that if "by any chance" Jekyll asks him into his private room, "don't go." This advice, along with Poole's barely controlled terror, unnerves Utterson.

The two men go to Dr. Jekyll's cabinet door in the laboratory.

Poole calls out that Utterson is here, asking to see the doctor. A strange voice within states that Jekyll will see no one. Politely, Poole says, "Thank you." Then, back in the kitchen, he asks Utterson, "Was that my master's voice?" Utterson grows pale. "It seems much changed," he says, trying to conceal his own fears. Poole is blunt. "Changed," he says, is hardly the word for "Jekyll's" voice. Poole says that he has worked for Jekyll for twenty years. The voice which they heard was *not* Dr. Jekyll's voice. Eight days ago, Poole says, he heard Jekyll cry out the name of God.

It is Poole's opinion that Dr. Jekyll was "made away with" at that time, and whoever is in the room now is "a thing known only to heaven."

Utterson tries his best to be rational about the mystery. Logically, he says, if someone *had* murdered Jekyll, why would he still be in there? Poole then explains more about whoever is in the room. "Whatever *it* is," he says, it "has been crying night after night for some sort of medicine." Earlier, Jekyll used to cry out for certain medicines and would write his orders on a sheet of paper and throw the paper on the stairs. For a week, there's been more papers on the stairs, a closed door, and whimpering. Poole has done his best to find the exact medicine, but no matter what he has brought back, it has not been "the right stuff." "It" always says that Poole has brought something that is "not pure" and, therefore, Poole has continued to receive orders to go on yet another errand to yet another store. "The drug is wanted bitter bad," Poole tells Utterson.

Utterson asks for some of these notes, and Poole is able to find one, crumpled up in one of his pockets. At first glance, the note seems to be merely a formal request – nothing amiss – asking that the pharmacist search for the drug "with the most sedulous care." Expense is no consideration, the note stresses, and there is a sense of urgency: "The importance of this to Dr. Jekyll can hardly be exaggerated." And then in a scribbled postscript, there is: "For God's sake, find me some of the old [drug]."

Utterson finally has to admit that this is indeed murky business. More than murky, says Poole: "I've seen *him*," he adds, referring to whoever lurks behind Jekyll's door. One day, Poole says, he came into the large room just below Jekyll's private room and there, digging among some crates, was a creature who was so startled at seeing Poole that he cried out "and whipped upstairs." If that *were* Jekyll, why did it run? Why did it "cry out like a rat"? And why did it wear a mask?

Ever the rational lawyer-sleuth, Utterson tries to explain to Poole that, to him, it seems as though Jekyll has been "seized with one of those maladies that both torture and deform the sufferer." The frantically sought-after drug, he hopes, is proof that Jekyll believes that "ultimate recovery" is possible.

Despite Utterson's rational explanations, Poole is not convinced: "That thing was not my master. . . . this was more of a dwarf. . . . do you think I do not know my master? . . . that thing was never Doctor Jekyll – God knows what it was, but it was never Doctor Jekyll." He is adamant: "In the belief of my heart . . . murder was done."

Utterson says that if Poole is convinced, then Utterson has no alternative: he considers it his duty to break down Jekyll's door, and Poole can use an ax which is in the surgery room, while Utterson will use the fireplace poker. Before they commence, though, they confess to one another that they both believe that *Hyde* is in the room and that it was he who killed Jekyll. They call Bradshaw, one of Jekyll's servants and tell him and a boy to watch the laboratory on the other side of the square. Then they set their watches. In ten minutes, they will assault the red blaize door of Dr. Jekyll's private room.

As the minutes pass, Jekyll's room grows quiet until all they can hear are soft, light footfalls, very different from Jekyll's heavy creaking tread, pacing to and fro. "An ill-conscience," Poole whispers, "there's blood foully shed." When ten minutes are up, a candle is set on the nearest table to give them more light. Then Utterson cries out: "Jekyll, I demand to see you."

The voice that answers Utterson pleads, "For God's sake, have mercy!" Utterson is stunned: the voice is *not* Jekyll's. *It belongs to Hyde.* Instantly, he calls out to Poole: "Down with the door!"

Poole crashes his ax four times against the sturdy red door, and each time, dismal, animal-like screeches are heard inside. On the fifth time, the lock bursts open, and the door falls inward. The scene inside is strange and incongruous. A quiet fire is flickering in the hearth, a tea kettle is singing, papers are neatly placed on the business table, and things are laid out for tea. Yet in the midst of this cozy scene, the body of a man is lying face down, terribly contorted and still twitching. The body is indeed dwarf-like, dressed in clothes far too large for him, clothes that would have fit Jekyll's large stature. Clearly, all life is gone, despite the fact that the muscles continue to twitch involuntarily. In one hand are the remains of a crushed vial. To Utterson, it seems to be a clear case of suicide. Sternly, he tells Poole that they have come too late to save or punish Hyde. Only one task remains now: they must find Jekyll's body.

They search the entire wing but find nothing: "nowhere was there any trace of Henry Jekyll, dead or alive." They go to the dissecting room and find Hyde's key, broken in half and rusty. The mystery remains. Once more they go up and view Hyde's dead body, then begin examining Jekyll's chemical equipment. Poole points out to Utterson the heaps of "white salt" that Jekyll had sent him on errands for.

The teapot suddenly boils over and startles them; Utterson picks up a pious work of literature and is aghast at the blasphemies written in the margin. The "cheval," the full-length mirror, puzzles both men. "This glass has seen some strange things," Poole whispers.

Examining Jekyll's business table, Utterson spies a large envelope with his name on it and unseals it; several enclosures fall to the floor. The first thing he reads is a will, a will very similar to the one which Jekyll left with Utterson earlier. However, this time, Utterson – and not Hyde – is designated as Jekyll's beneficiary. For a moment, Utterson is dazed. *Why* would Jekyll make out a new will? Utterson knows that he has nagged and reprimanded Jekyll excessively in the past. Surely Jekyll was angry at Utterson for being so demanding. Yet why did Jekyll make Utterson his beneficiary?

Utterson then examines another piece of paper. Shouting at Poole, he is delighted to recognize the doctor's handwriting and the date at the top of the note: Jekyll "was alive and here this day," he cries. Surely, Utterson thinks, the doctor must *still* be alive; perhaps he has fled. With great anxiety, he decides to read the next enclosure.

The message is brief. Jekyll has disappeared, under circumstances that he had the "penetration to foresee." However, his end, he fears, is certain. He asks Utterson to read Dr. Lanyon's note first, for Lanyon has told Jekyll that his note is now in Utterson's possession. If after reading Lanyon's narrative, there are still unanswered questions, Utterson is then to read the large, sealed packet containing Jekyll's "confession."

Utterson turns to Poole and asks him to say nothing of this sealed packet; perhaps they can yet save Jekyll's reputation. Glancing at a clock, he sees that it is ten o'clock. He will go home, read the documents, return before midnight, and then they will send for the police.

Commentary

Chapter 8 functions as perhaps the most traditional narrative chapter in the novel. Most of the other chapters present *incidents*: "Story [or Incident] of the Door," "Incident of the Letter," "Remarkable Incident of Dr. Lanyon," and "Incident at the Window"; the other chapters, similarly, give accounts of wills, what is reported in the newspapers, Dr. Lanyon's "Account," and finally Dr. Jekyll's own "Statement." In contrast, this chapter flies along in its narrative sequences with such varied activities as the gathering of forces within Jekyll's house (and note how frightened all the servants are: some, like the maid, succumb to hysterics; likewise, all stand "huddled together like a flock of sheep"). They are terrified of what Mr. Hyde stands for and are afraid that he might appear. Then, in swift succession, there is the breaking down of Jekyll's door, the discovery of the dead body of Edward Hyde, the frantic search for Dr. Jekyll, the discovery of the new will, the new note, and Dr. Jekyll's final statement. In other words, whereas many of the other chapters concern themselves with only one single incident, this chapter is crowded with *many* incidents.

The beginning of the chapter is rather slow because the distraught Poole is not educated enough to convince Utterson of the seriousness of the strange events occurring in Dr. Jekyll's laboratory. We should note the long, laborious method by which Utterson is finally convinced. That is, each time Poole offers some information, Utterson is able to offer some rational explanation; he sees the faithful Poole as merely a superstitious servant.

Utterson is not yet ready to act, but when Poole exposes Utterson to the sound of the voice behind the door, Utterson acknowledges that a change has indeed occurred. Then, when Utterson is told about Poole's hearing a cry of despair eight days ago, about the continual crying night and day, about the desperate need for some chemicals and some drugs, about the glimpse of the strange man in the laboratory, about the weeping of a seemingly lost soul, and about the dwarfish figure that Poole believes to be that of Edward Hyde, Utterson is at last ready to act.

After breaking the door down and upon seeing the dead person (a suicide) in the laboratory, Utterson and we, the readers, still think that the dead person is Edward Hyde, even though the "clothes were far too large for him, clothes of the doctor's bigness." In addition, Utterson's puzzlement over why such an evil person would commit suicide adds to the mystery. Then the mystery of the duality is increased by Utterson's assumption that Hyde has murdered Dr. Jekyll. The search for Jekyll's body still leaves the reader in suspense over the Jekyll/Hyde dichotomy or duality, especially when the search for Dr. Jekyll's body is, of course, futile: "Nowhere was there any trace of Henry Jekyll, dead or alive."

The discovery of the broken key and the rusty "fractures" (door or key openings) suggests that Jekyll's rational actions have allowed him to arrange his living accommodations so that Hyde has been prevented from going out the back door. He could not leave by the front door because since the murder of Sir Danvers, he would have been apprehended by, or at least reported by, the servants. Thus, even at the most insane end of his life, Jekyll retains enough of his old rational self to keep Hyde in bounds.

As Utterson and Poole examine Dr. Jekyll's laboratory quarters, more evidence of the Jekyll/Hyde duality is found. For example, they find a pious book which Jekyll had held in great esteem, "annotated in his own hand with startling blasphemies." But, of course, Utterson is misled here. Had he remembered his assistant's, Mr. Guest's, analysis of handwriting—that Hyde's and Jekyll's handwriting was virtually the same except for a slightly different slope—then he would have realized that the vulgar and blasphemous annotations were made by Hyde—not Jekyll—and yet they are the same, thus emphasizing, ironically, the duality of man.

The entire mystery reaches its apex at the end of this chapter with the discovery of Dr. Jekyll's new will, making Gabriel John Utterson Jekyll's sole beneficiary. The name of Edward Hyde is struck out. Utterson's confusion is that the vile, evil Hyde was obviously there in the laboratory, saw the change in the will, and yet did nothing. Furthermore, by the date of the brief note—dated that day—Utterson is totally confused, because of the realization that earlier in the day, Jekyll was still alive. Finally, in the note which Jekyll left to Utterson, the word "disappeared" appears again: "When this shall fall into your hands, I shall have disappeared." This same word appeared in Jekyll's original will, as well as in Dr. Lanyon's instructions to Utterson, and now it appears again in this letter. Therefore, Utterson is utterly confused. And since the final two chapters are "documents," and we neither see nor hear anymore from Utterson, we can only speculate as to how this strange information from his two closest friends will affect him.

CHAPTER 9

"Doctor Lanyon's Narrative"

On the night of January 9, Lanyon writes, I received a registered letter. Immediately, I recognized the handwriting of my old school-companion Henry Jekyll on the envelope. This surprised me. Henry and I weren't in the habit of corresponding; after all, we both live in London and I had just seen him the night before at one of his dinner parties. Whatever could be the reason for such a formality as sending a registered letter? My curiosity was high.

> Dear Lanyon [writes Jekyll],
>
> Despite the fact that we have differed on scientific matters in the past, you are one of my oldest friends, and that is why I am asking you to do a favor for me. It is a favor on which my honor rests. If you fail me, I am lost.
>
> Please help me. Take a cab to my house, Poole will let you in, and then go to my room. If the door is locked, force it open. Open the drawer marked "E" (force the lock if necessary), and take out all its contents—some powders, a vial, and a paper book. Take everything home with you. Then, at midnight, a man will arrive at your house, ordered to do so by me. Give him the drawer you took from my room. That is all. If you do this, you will have earned my complete gratitude. I know that what I am asking borders on the fantastic, but if you fail to carry it out, either my death or my madness will be on your conscience. I tremble at the thought that you might fail

me. If you do this, however, my troubles will be over.

Your friend,

H. J.

P.S. If the postoffice fails to deliver this on schedule, do as I ask anyway. Expect my messenger at midnight. It may be too late; I cannot say. If it is, you will have seen the last of Henry Jekyll.

After I finished reading Jekyll's letter, I reflected on the possibility that Dr. Jekyll was insane. Yet until that was proved, I felt bound to do what my old friend asked me to do. Thus, I went immediately to Jekyll's house; a locksmith had been called and after two hours, the door to Jekyll's private study was opened. I took out the drawer described in Jekyll's letter, tied it carefully in a sheet, and returned home with it. There, I examined it carefully. What I found whetted my curiosity, but it told me little that was definite. There was a simple-looking sort of salt, a vial half-full of blood-red, highly pungent liquor, and the notebook contained little – a series of dates, covering a period of many years, which ceased quite abruptly nearly a year go. A few brief remarks were beside the dates; the word "double" occurred perhaps six times in a total of several hundred entries and once, very early in the list, were the words, "total failure," followed by several exclamation marks. For the life of me, I couldn't imagine how any of this could affect the honor, the sanity, or the life of my old friend Dr. Jekyll. And why all the secrecy? The more I thought about it, I wondered if Jekyll might not be suffering from some sort of cerebral disease. Yet I was determined to do as he asked – but not before loading my old revolver.

At midnight, the knocker on my door sounded very gently. Outside was a small man crouching against one of the porch pillars. I asked him if he was Jekyll's agent. He gestured a tortured "yes" and, looking furtively behind him, slipped inside. Keeping a hand on my revolver, I took a close look at the small man. I had never seen him before. He was certainly a distasteful creature; his face jerked in convulsions, he seemed physically ill, and as a doctor, I wondered about these symptoms. His clothes, which were obviously expensive, were much too large for him. His trousers were rolled up ridiculously, and the waist of his coat fell below his hips. Under other circumstances, I would have laughed at his clown-like appearance, but this man was clearly abnormal, disgustingly so. Again, as a medical man, I couldn't help being curious about his origin, his life, and his livelihood.

The strange little man was unusually excited, asking again and again if I had "it." I tried to calm him, but he seemed to be on the verge of hysteria, so I pointed to where it lay, on the floor behind a table. Instantly, he sprang on it, then laid his hand on his heart, and I could hear his teeth grate and his jaws convulse. Then he began mixing the powders with the liquid, which changed colors before my eyes. I was fascinated, and he noted this and asked, "Will you be wise? Will you be guided? I can take this glass and leave. Or I can swallow it before you and show you a new land of knowledge, new paths to fame. What you see will stagger the Devil himself."

I confess that my curiosity again got the best of me. I asked him to continue. He agreed but reminded me of my professional vows and of my deep-rooted belief in traditional medicine, for what I was about to see would be a wonder from the realm of *transcendental* medicine.

Then he drank the potion in one long swallow and cried out, reeled, staggered, clutched at the table, and suddenly his face became black, his features began to melt, and in the next moment, Henry Jekyll stood before me.

What he told me during the next hour, I cannot bring myself to put on paper. I can only relate what I saw and how my soul was sickened. I ask myself if I believe it, and I cannot answer. Terror haunts me constantly. My faith in medicine and mankind has been sundered. I feel my days are numbered. Only one thing remains to be said. That "creature" who came on an errand for Jekyll, by Jekyll's own admission, was none other than Edward Hyde, the murderer of Sir Danvers Carew!

Commentary

In terms of the narrative structure of the novel, finally and for the first time, the reader comes to the astounding realization that (1) Dr. Jekyll and Mr. Hyde are one and the same person; or (2) Dr. Jekyll and Mr. Hyde are two parts of the same person, one evil and the other good; or (3) Mr. Hyde is a part of Dr. Jekyll, that diminished part that represents the evil in all of us. There could be other options in addition to the above, but these are the most traditional.

Likewise, in terms of the narrative structure, this information comes to us in the form of a long narrative set forth by Dr. Lanyon, but we should also be aware that Dr. Lanyon does not tell us *every-thing*: when Hyde has drunk the potion and has again become Jekyll, the two "old friends" apparently talked for an hour, but Dr. Lanyon writes, "What he [Jekyll] told me in the next hour, I cannot bring my mind to set on paper." Therefore, the reader does not yet have the complete story, because the timid, shocked, and horrified Dr. Lanyon is too stricken by the implications of Jekyll's story to even write it down.

We should remember from Chapter 6 that on the 8th of January, Lanyon, along with Utterson and others, dined at Dr. Jekyll's house; then on the 9th of January, Dr. Lanyon received the note from Dr. Jekyll (dated the 10th of December, an error of consistency on Stevenson's part), a note in which Jekyll, in the person of Hyde, pleads with his old friend for help; now we realize this will be a type of help which will finally bring Lanyon into direct contact with Jekyll's theories, which Lanyon has so long rejected. The direct confrontation will be in the person of Edward Hyde, with his sinister and evil ways. And true to form, Lanyon's initial reaction to Hyde is the same as the reaction of others – "There was something abnormal and misbegotten in the very essence of the creature."

When Hyde has received the chemicals from Dr. Lanyon and has mixed the infamous potion, he taunts Lanyon with a challenge: shall he (Hyde) leave now, with Lanyon still in ignorance, or does Lanyon have "the greed of curiosity"? If Hyde stays, then "a new province of knowledge and new avenues to fame and power shall be laid open to you, here, in this room, upon the instant; and your sight shall be blasted by a prodigy to stagger the unbelief of Satan." We must first question how this revelation will open up new avenues of "fame and power" to Lanyon – especially since the same knowledge has destroyed Jekyll. But we must remember that it is *not Jekyll* who is offering Lanyon this awful challenge – it is, ironically, *Hyde*, and he wants revenge for the many times that Lanyon has ridiculed Jekyll for being "too fanciful" and "too metaphysical" and for being interested in such "unscientific balderdash." Finally, Lanyon is to see with his own eyes

what he has so long rejected and ridiculed. The entire person of Jekyll/
Hyde would, of course, not taunt the good Dr. Lanyon, but the evil,
malicious, and vindictive Hyde takes great, perverse pleasure in taunt-
ing Lanyon.

Lanyon assents, and Hyde drinks the potion. What happens to
Hyde is a delightful challenge to filmmakers and is vividly described
by Stevenson: "A cry followed: he reeled, staggered, clutched at the
table, and held on, staring with injected eyes, gasping with open
mouth. . . . He seemed to swell – his face became suddenly black and
the features seem to melt and alter." The effect of this scene destroys
Lanyon, for as we saw in Chapter 6, Dr. Lanyon is dead three weeks
after this scene. Observing the metamorphosis, Lanyon can only
scream, "Oh God . . . Oh God" again and again as he watches Hyde
become Jekyll. Thus Hyde and, ultimately, Jekyll both have their
revenge.

The horror of the transformation is not, we assume, the only thing
that kills Lanyon. After the transformation, Jekyll talks to Lanyon for
an hour, and we must assume that he tells Lanyon everything that
we hear in Chapter 10. The point is that Lanyon cannot tolerate the
idea that man has an evil nature, and yet he has just been exposed
to the incontrovertible proof that man does indeed possess an actual
evil nature which *can* be isolated from his dual-natured self. As we
noted earlier, the actual horror of the discovery that Jekyll and Hyde
are one and the same person lies not in the transformation itself but
in the full realization concerning the nature of evil found in all men
because Hyde has stood before Lanyon as EVIL INCARNATE. And this
is followed by Jekyll's long explanation which Lanyon "cannot bring
[his] mind to set on paper." For upon hearing Jekyll's story, Lanyon's
"soul sickened. . . . My life was shaken to its roots; sleep has left me;
the deadliest terror sits by me at all hours. . . . I feel that I must die."
Thus, the deadliest terror that Lanyon fears must be the fear that *his*
own evil nature will emerge, and for a prominent man who has lived
an exemplary, mild, and meek life while attaining fame, this possibility
is simply too much; it destroys him. But before it destroys him, he
completely rejects not just Hyde, but Jekyll also – in his entirety. As
Lanyon said in Chapter 6, "I wish to see or hear no more of Dr. Jekyll.
. . . I am quite done with that person; and I beg that you will spare
me any allusions to one whom I regard as dead." Thus, we now know
that the horror of the discovery that Jekyll and Hyde are one person

results in the discovery that Lanyon himself is also part evil. To escape thinking further about this self-realization, Lanyon therefore rejects Dr. Jekyll – as well as himself – because he has not the strength to struggle with evil. The knowledge of this phenomenon simply kills him.

CHAPTER 10

"Jekyll's Full Statement"

I was born [writes Jekyll] to a wealthy family and, after a good education, I gained the respect of all who knew me. I seemed to be guaranteed an honorable and distinguished future. If I had any single, serious flaw, it was that I was perhaps inclined to be a bit too spirited. Other people admired my light-hearted good nature, but personally, I was annoyed by it. I preferred to present an unchanging seriousness to the public. For that reason, I willfully decided to conceal *all* my pleasures. Now, years later, I realize that my life has been an admirable one, but it has certainly been a fraudulent one. No one but me knows my true nature. All these years, the public has seen only a veneer of my real self. No one could guess what degrading things I have done secretly, things which I must say in all honesty, I enjoyed very much. And yet I do *not* consider myself a hypocrite, for man has a dual nature. The professional, respectable side of my character is as much a part of me as is the side that has enjoyed to the fullest my secret "irregularities."

Because I knew, first-hand, about my own – and man's – dual nature, my medical studies began to increasingly focus on the origins and dimensions of this phenomenon of duality. This investigation, of course, bordered on the mystical and the transcendental, but only these disciplines could help me better understand myself and the duality of all human beings.

What I hoped to do, eventually, was to separate these two sides of a person's character. I reasoned with myself that if I could do this, then I could eradicate the unhappiness that exists in the "darker self," the self that so often makes life seem unbearable. I saw my quest as humanistic, for if I achieved my goal, man might walk more securely "on the upward path" and no longer be exposed to the disgrace of evil.

To me, the curse of mankind seemed to be that man should have two separate natures within himself, forces which were continually struggling with one another. Thus, I began to speculate that our so-called "solid" body might not be so solid, after all. If one could find the physical or psychic membrane that bound our duality, it would be possible to sever it. But because I attempted to rid man of "the bad seed" that resides in him, I find now to my sorrow that such a task is impossible. My discovery remains incomplete. I feel now that man is doomed to lead a life which will always be a life of burden.

However, I tell myself, I *tried* to remove that burden, and I *was* able to discover a drug that could extract the "lower elements" of myself. Moreover, I was able to look upon this "self" and see that it, while ignoble, was a part of myself, therefore "natural."

I want you to know that I did nothing rashly. I attempted my experiment only after much consideration, for I knew that I was risking death by using so potent a drug as I had devised. But it was my extreme scientific curiosity that tempted me to try and reach into the unknown and shatter the theory that man was indivisible. I was sure that human beings had at least two distinct entities – a good self and an evil self. My task was to use my body for my experiment and try to extract my "evil" self.

I well remember the night I took the potion. I had bought a large quantity of a particular salt that I knew would be the key catalyst; I mixed it with the other ingredients and watched them boil and smoke and then, summoning up all the courage I had, I drank the potion. It began working almost immediately: a grinding tore at my bones, I was racked with deadly nausea, and when my mind cleared, I felt strangely younger, lighter, and happier. I felt newborn, and, above all, absolutely free! I had no conscience. I was evil and wicked with no constraints.

I stretched my hands out in joy and was suddenly aware that not only had I changed inwardly, but that I had changed physically. I had become stunted. Desperately, I sought a mirror and dashed from the laboratory, ran across the courtyard and into my bedroom, where there was a mirror. There, for the first time, I saw my evil side, Edward Hyde, sickly and deformed, despite the fact that I seemingly felt younger and happier. I realized, of course, that my "professional" self had been rigorously trained. This "side" of myself which I now saw had been kept secret for many, many years in the dark cellar of my soul. No wonder it looked sickly and less developed. Studying

Hyde's face in the mirror, I was horrified to recall the aura of "goodness" that continually emanated from Jekyll's face, whereas evil positively colored the entire countenance of Edward Hyde. Yet I was not entirely repelled by what I saw, for this was me, or at least a part of me. What I saw in the mirror seemed natural and human.

I did not linger at the mirror. I had to complete my experiment. Therefore, I rushed to my laboratory, prepared the potion again, and regained the self known to the world as Henry Jekyll, a dual-natured man, wholly unlike the one-dimensional, wholly evil man whom I had been only moments earlier. It occurred to me then that the evil within me was, or might be, stronger than the good, but I dismissed the thought. After all, my potion was neutral. Had I wished to release my pure, wholly saint-like qualities, I could have. But I chose, instead, to extract the evil side of my nature and I had, in the process, given birth to the wholly evil Edward Hyde.

My discovery, though, was dangerous because now, I was growing old. I *liked* feeling young and free. Thus, I was increasingly tempted to drink the potion and drop the dull body of the aging Dr. Jekyll and become, instead, the lithe, young Edward Hyde. In fact, I liked Hyde so much that I furnished a house and hired a discreet but unscrupulous housekeeper for him. Then I announced to my servants that Mr. Hyde was to have free liberty and power in my house. It was a queer, perverse sort of joy to call at my own home in the body of Hyde and watch the reactions of the servants. My next task was to make Hyde my beneficiary in case anything should happen, accidentally, to Jekyll during one of the experiments.

Hyde was a rare luxury. Other men had to hire professional villains to carry out their crimes and also risk a bad conscience afterward, in addition to blackmail. I was safe. Edward Hyde could enjoy all my wicked pleasures and execute all of my angry, vengeful, irrational wishes — and he would be free from shame, for he was free from conscience. He was truly evil. *I*, Jekyll, however, did have a sense of objectivity, and often I was awed at the utter depravity of Hyde. Yet even if I was aghast at Hyde's sensual debauchery, his acts were beyond all "natural" laws, as was I. Thus, my conscience relaxed. It was Hyde, not I, who was guilty. Jekyll's good qualities remained fresh and intact each morning after Hyde had spent an entire night in drunken, bestial orgies of lust and violence. And then, finally, my own conscience — that is, Jekyll's — did not merely "relax"; it slept.

I will not go into the details of Hyde's depravity, except to mention that one night he accidentally ran headlong into a child, and the mishap drew a crowd. Coincidentally, Utterson, among the people who gathered was a kinsman of yours. For the first time, I feared for my life, and in order to pacify the child's family, I had no alternative but to open the door to the dissecting room, go inside, and write a check on Jekyll's account. Later, I prudently set up a separate checking account for Hyde and had him use a backhand script when necessary. I thought that I had taken sufficient precautions to furnish safety for Hyde, but some two months before Sir Danvers Carew was murdered, a terrifying thing occurred. I awoke and realized that I was not Jekyll. I thought that I had gone to bed in my own body in my own room, but I could not be sure, for I realized that I had awakened in the small, misshapen body of Hyde.

I rushed to the mirror in absolute terror. It was Hyde whom I saw. Somehow, during the night, my body chemistry had reversed itself, and the evil Hyde had taken possession of me. I had no alternative but to dash through the courtyard and the corridors and see one of my servants look in wonder at Hyde's appearance in my house at such an early hour.

Ten minutes later, I was Jekyll again. I made a pretense of eating breakfast, but I was not hungry. I feared that I was losing the power to choose when I wished to change myself into Hyde. Hyde was now making that decision. Accordingly, it became necessary for me to double, then triple, the dosage of the drug in order to keep Hyde in check. And not knowing what side effects the drug might have, I knew that I was risking death. But I had no choice. *I* had to control Hyde. My "better" self was losing not only the power to return to its former self, but I realized that I, Jekyll, was losing the *will* to do so. Soon I was faced with a dilemma. Which person did I want to be ? The free, conscience-less Hyde? Or the "good," suppressed Doctor Jekyll? If I remained Jekyll forever, I could never more enjoy the depravities that Hyde gorged himself on. I would be, once more, a good man, but I would be a sterile shell of a man, constantly fighting the fires of temptation because I had tasted – and reveled in – sin, with no remorse or shame.

Rationally, I chose to remain Jekyll, and I said farewell, I thought, to the secret pleasures of the free soul, Edward Hyde. But my decision wasn't one of total commitment. I didn't do away with Hyde's apartment or his clothes—despite the fact that for two months, I led an exemplary life. Then, without warning one day, I was tortured with throbbing knots of lust and depravity. Hyde was struggling to be released. And in a moment of weakness, I gave him his freedom. I drank the potion and once more, Edward Hyde was freed. He had been caged for so long that he came out roaring, and one of his first acts was to savagely murder Sir Danvers Carew.

When I was able to transform myself once more into Jekyll, I broke Hyde's key to the dissecting room and stamped it under my heel. I was finished with Hyde. Yet one day while I was in Regent's Park enjoying the sun, I began to feel my body change of its own will. I became Hyde. The only solution was to flee to a hotel and write a letter to Lanyon and one to Poole in order to obtain the ingredients for the potion so that I could become Jekyll once more.

I was able to accomplish this, but Lanyon of course was horrified to see Hyde change into the body of Jekyll before his eyes. Yet his horror did not match my own horror later, for Hyde increasingly began to take possession of me. If I slept or dozed, I awoke as Hyde and I was doomed. I was no longer able to control Hyde.

Today, Hyde still controls me. And he despises me. He fears the gallows and so he must dash back into Jekyll's body for safety, but he does so resentfully, and he takes out his raging hate by scribbling blasphemies in the margins of my books. He even destroyed the portrait of my father. But how can I kill Hyde? He loves his freedom so. I no longer have the old powders for the potion. Poole has been unable to obtain any that are effective. Whatever I used originally must have had an unknown impurity that allowed me to release Hyde. Thus, I now must end my narrative—as Jekyll. Yet if while writing this, Hyde surfaces, he will tear it to pieces. Hopefully, I can finish and save it for you, Utterson, so that you can begin to understand my strange history. Will Hyde die on the gallows? I no longer have the power to control or foresee either my own destiny or Hyde's. This is truly my hour of death!

Commentary

In Chapter 8, Henry Jekyll referred to his document which constitutes the entirety of Chapter 10 as "the *confession* of your unworthy and unhappy friend—Henry Jekyll," yet this final chapter refers to the document as a "full statement." This statement, then, gives us an account of Dr. Jekyll's experiments and along with the preceding chapter, it constitutes what the average person considers as the entire Jekyll/Hyde story.

In giving us his background, Jekyll constantly emphasizes the excellence of his background which commands the respect of all; his honorable conduct is exemplary to the world, when contrasted with the "blazon irregularities" which he hid with a morbid sense of shame. Thus, early in Jekyll's life, he recognized a "profound duplicity of life . . . so profound a *double* dealer." He also recognized early "that man is not truly one, but truly two," and then he acknowledged "the thorough and primitive duality of man." Also, very early, he saw the need to hide the shameful part of himself from the world, and the necessity to try and separate the two selves.

Note here that many critics are not content to interpret the novel as a conflict between good (Jekyll) and evil (Hyde), but, instead, the novel points out, according to them, that evil (represented by Hyde) is only a small portion of man, a portion represented by Hyde's diminutive and dwarfish size. Certainly, Dr. Jekyll implies this when he theorizes that "man will be ultimately known for a mere polity of multifarious, incongruous, and independent denizens"—that is, evil and good and many other qualities will ultimately be found to make up the entire man. However, Jekyll and his experiments can only prove at the present moment that man's existence has two parts— one good and one evil. Jekyll's experiment, which Lanyon found so horrifying, was an attempt to separate the two components, and when he discovered the correct formula and drank it, Jekyll was approaching a robust fifty years of age; yet after his transformation into Edward Hyde, he felt younger, lighter, and more sensual. He knew from the beginning that he was "tenfold more wicked [and] evil."

As often noted in the above commentaries, after the transformation to Hyde, Jekyll "had lost in stature." He was much smaller as "the evil side of [his] nature . . . was less robust and less developed than the good." This observation obviously contradicts the critics who see Jekyll/Hyde as being ½ good and ½ evil. Hyde, therefore, as the evil part of man, is *less* than the total man, but he is nevertheless an important part of the total man. This is represented in the scene when Hyde looks in the mirror and sees himself as "natural and human": he was "conscious of no repugnance, rather a leap of welcome." This is, of course, because Jekyll sees Hyde as a part of himself. And yet, from Chapter 1 onward, everyone who encounters Hyde is utterly horrified and repulsed by his pure evil. Ultimately, Jekyll himself will come to look upon Hyde as his "errant son" who must be punished.

As Hyde, then, all sorts of pleasures were indulged in. It is never mentioned what the exact nature of all the secret, depraved, disreputable acts was, but most people (perhaps because of the movie versions of this novel) consider these "vulgar" acts to have something to do with sex. In the minds of the late Victorians (late nineteenth century), evil and sex were synonymous, and certainly to such a highly respectable and eminent man as Dr. Jekyll, it would have been extremely disgraceful if he were to have been discovered in some sort of illicit sex. Of course, we know that, as Hyde, he did murder Sir Danvers without provocation, but no other crimes were ever attributed to him; after the murder, however, all sorts of tales surfaced concerning his disreputable life and his vile actions. Therefore, since he was never charged with any other specific crime, most readers do assume that his vileness, vulgarity, and villainy were associated with sexual matters – matters which a dignified and respectable scientist could not be associated with, but activities which he, as Jekyll, had pursued in his early youth and now could once more enjoy in the person of Hyde, while the respectable Jekyll remained perfectly safe from detection. Even after the murder of Sir Danvers, and Jekyll vows to give up the "liberty, the comparative youth, the light step, leaping impulses, and secret pleasures that I had *enjoyed* in the disguise of Hyde," the extreme enjoyment he receives as Hyde is ultimately why Jekyll cannot put Hyde aside. Jekyll thoroughly enjoys, vicariously, the multifarious, decadent activities performed by his double.

Thus, Jekyll's enjoyment of Hyde's activities allows Hyde to grow in stature, and of the two men, Hyde is slowly gaining the ascendancy over Jekyll. The mere fact that Jekyll never gave up the house in Soho (rented for Hyde) nor destroyed Hyde's clothes is proof to us that the vow he made to Utterson in Chapter 5, after the murder of Sir Danvers ("I swear to God I will never set eyes on him again. I bind my honor to you that I am done with him"), was indeed a hypocritical or empty vow. Even though Jekyll did try for two months to lead a "life of such severity," the Hyde in Jekyll was constantly struggling for release. Repressed for so long, when Hyde emerged, he "came out roaring." Jekyll now has to contend with his "lust of evil," with the "damned horrors of the evenings," and with"the ugly face of iniquity" which stared into his soul. Hyde is not to be denied because, secretly, Jekyll still desires his presence and his activities. But he also knows that if he lets "Hyde peep out an instant . . . the hands of all men would be raised to take and slay him." Therefore, Hyde is trapped by his own evil ways and is confined to the laboratory.

However, when Jekyll is sitting peacefully one day in Regent's Park, in broad daylight, he feels all of the symptoms of Hyde emerging without the aid of the chemical potion. Hyde appears because Jekyll, who has so long tried to deny and suppress him, subconsciously desires that he appear again. But the appearance must be concealed, and so Jekyll/Hyde – by now, it is difficult to separate the two – conceive of a plan to get their revenge on Dr. Lanyon, who has so often ridiculed Dr. Jekyll and has refused to even contemplate the possibility of an evil side of his nature existing. Thus, the elaborate scheme involving Lanyon – the letter written by Hyde, but in Jekyll's handwriting – allows Jekyll/Hyde to achieve their revenge against Dr. Lanyon.

From this point on, until Utterson and Poole break down the door, Jekyll/Hyde have an even stranger relationship with each other. Jekyll hates Hyde for the ascendancy that Hyde has over him, and Hyde hates Jekyll both because of Jekyll's hatred, but more importantly because Hyde knows that Jekyll can destroy him (Hyde) by committing suicide as Jekyll. The final irony is that Jekyll is the one who commits suicide (the evil Hyde, of course, would never do this), but during the act of Jekyll's dying, Hyde regains the ascendancy so that Utterson and Poole find not the body of Jekyll, but that of Hyde.

CHARACTER ANALYSES

Dr. Henry (Harry) Jekyll

A prominent, popular London scientist, who is well known for his dinner parties, Jekyll is a large, handsome man of perhaps fifty. He owns a large estate and has recently drawn up his will, leaving his immense fortune to a man whom Jekyll's lawyer, Utterson, thoroughly disapproves of.

Jekyll's own story of his life is recorded in his "Statement," which comprises the entirety of Chapter 10. He was born to a good family, had a good education, and was respected by all who knew him. As a youth, he thinks that perhaps he was too light-hearted. He confesses to many youthful indiscretions, which he says that he enjoyed very much – indiscretions which he was very careful to keep secret. However, there came a time when he realized that his professional career could be ruined if one of these indiscretions were to be exposed, and so he repressed them.

Now, however, that he is middle-aged, he has been fascinated with the theory that man has a "good" side and a "bad" side, and he has decided to investigate the theory. His investigations were successful; he compounded a potion that could release the "evil" in a person in the form of an entirely different physical person, one who would take over one's own body and soul. Then one could commit acts of evil and feel no guilt; furthermore, one could drink the same potion and be transformed back into one's original self.

Jekyll's evil dimension took the form of Edward Hyde, a man who committed any number of crimes and performed acts of sexual perversion; seemingly, his most serious crime is the vicious murder of Sir Danvers Carew, a Member of Parliament.

Jekyll's fascination with his "other" self became so obsessive that he was finally no longer able to control the metamorphosis process, and Edward Hyde began appearing whenever *he* wanted to – and not at the command of Dr. Jekyll. Jekyll became, therefore, a frightened recluse, trying desperately to control Hyde, but successively failing, especially whenever he would doze off. Finally, crazed by anxiety and a lack of sleep, he hears Utterson and Poole, his butler, breaking down his private study door and, in desperation, he commits suicide, but just as he loses consciousness, Hyde appears, and it is the writhing body of the dying Hyde which Utterson and Poole discover.

Edward Hyde

Hyde, as his name indicates, represents the fleshy (sexual) aspect of man which the Victorians felt the need to "hide" – as Utterson once punned on his name: "Well, if he is Mr. Hyde, I will be Mr. Seek."

Hyde actually comes to represent the embodiment of pure evil merely for the sake of evil. When he is first extracted and in our first encounter with him, he is seen running over a young girl, simply trampling on her. He does not do this out of spite – or intentionally; it is simply an amoral act. He does make reparations. But even in this first encounter, he raises a fear, an antagonism, and a deep loathing in other people. The reaction of others to him is one of horror, partly because while looking at him, others feel a deep desire to strike out at him and kill him. In other words, his mere physical appearance brings out the very worst evil in other people.

Since Hyde represents the purely evil in man (or in Dr. Jekyll), he is, therefore, symbolically represented as being much smaller than Dr. Jekyll – Jekyll's clothes are far too large for him – and Hyde is also many years younger than Jekyll, symbolically suggesting that the evil side of Jekyll did not develop until years after he was born.

Hyde also creates terror; the servants are extremely frightened of him. When they think he is around the house, the servants cringe in horror, and some go into hysterics.

As the novel progresses, Hyde's evil becomes more and more pronounced. He bludgeons Sir Danvers Carew to death for absolutely no reason other than the fact that Sir Danvers appeared to be a good and kindly man – and pure evil detests pure goodness.

Since Hyde represents the evil or perverse side of Jekyll, and since Jekyll does, vicariously, enjoy the degradations which Hyde commits, Hyde gradually begins to take the ascendancy over the good Dr. Jekyll.

A conflict between them erupts, as though the older Dr. Jekyll is a father to the errant and prodigal son. He wants to punish this son, but at the same time, he recognizes that Hyde is an intimate part of himself. Ultimately, when Jekyll commits suicide in order to get rid of Hyde (suicide is an evil act in the eyes of the church), this allows Hyde to become the dominant evil figure, and the dying Jekyll becomes Hyde in the final death throes.

Gabriel John Utterson

Except for the last two chapters, most of the rest of the novel is seen through the eyes of Mr. Utterson, who functions as the "eyes" of "conscience" through which we, the readers, evaluate most of the novel. Therefore, if Utterson is deceived in his opinion of some event, then the reader is likewise deceived. This is because Utterson is such a fine, objective narrator who represents a highly moral and upright person; thus, we believe all that he says, and since he is a man of such prominence and integrity, we cannot doubt his explanation or his view of any event.

Utterson is a strange case of opposites. We first hear that he has a fondness for wine but mortifies himself with gin instead. This, at first, sounds weird for a moral narrator, but then we are told that he is not censorious – that is, he is not anxious to judge and condemn his fellow man. This allows many people of differing degrees to come to him to seek advice, and it allows him to be privy to the secrets of the great and the less great. Yet, he also possesses an intense loyalty to his friends and is constantly concerned for their welfare. This attribute allows him to be deeply distressed over Dr. Jekyll's relationship with Mr. Edward Hyde. That is, Utterson is a shrewd judge of character, and he sees in Edward Hyde an immoral and evil person, and he is deeply concerned for his friend's (Dr. Jekyll's) well-being.

For example, when he is convinced that Edward Hyde has injured Dr. Jekyll, he is quick to take action and break down the door to the laboratory in order to come to his friend's aid.

Utterson is also the type of person who inspires trust – and deservedly so. When his friend Dr. Lanyon leaves a note not to be opened until Dr. Jekyll's death or disappearance, he is tempted to read it in order to see if there is any information which will assist Dr. Jekyll. Yet his honor forces him to store the document away without reading it.

Ultimately, we do not know how Utterson is affected by the revelation found in Dr. Lanyon's and Dr. Jekyll's confessions, but from the horror of seeing Dr. Jekyll at the window, when Dr. Jekyll apparently began changing into Hyde, we can assume that Utterson was deeply affected, but due to his objective control over life and its vicissitudes – as a lawyer he has seen all types of criminals – we can assume that, unlike Dr. Lanyon, Utterson was able to survive.

Dr. Hastie Lanyon

In contrast to Jekyll, the "metaphysical" scientist and his interest in releasing "evil" spirits which become physically alive, taking over the body and soul of their owner and embodying it in their own misshapen representations, Lanyon is a "traditional" scientist – completely uninterested in "the other world." Once, Lanyon and Jekyll were fast friends, but when Jekyll became too fascinated with delving

into the darker aspects of science, Lanyon broke off their friendship –
about ten years before the novel begins.

Lanyon is questioned keenly by Utterson about Jekyll, but Lanyon
will say nothing definite, just that Jekyll is interested in the perverse
aspects of science, and for that reason, he is no longer friends with
him.

Finally, Jekyll/Hyde decide to take their revenge on Lanyon for
his prudish denunciations of Jekyll; Hyde arranges a metamorphosis
to occur before the good doctor Lanyon. Lanyon is so horrified that
Jekyll has been successful in releasing his own evil that Lanyon cannot
face the thought that there resides a similar Edward Hyde within him;
three weeks after Hyde's contrived baiting of Lanyon's curiosity, the
meek doctor is dead of shock.

QUESTIONS FOR REVIEW

1. What is the nature of the relationship between Mr. Utterson and
   Mr. Enfield?

2. How is Jekyll's house and laboratory physically situated so as to
   suggest a symbolic significance to the arrangement?

3. After reading the first chapter, how do you account for the reader's
   intense interest in such an evil man as Edward Hyde?

4. Describe the basic physical appearance of Henry Jekyll, and then
   describe the physical appearance of Edward Hyde.

5. What qualities does Mr. Utterson possess that make him such
   an excellent narrator, or the "central intelligence," or "consciousness" through which most of the novel is presented?

6. Discuss the significance of the names of Utterson, Jekyll and
   Hyde.

7. Discuss Jekyll's and Lanyon's relationship with one another.

8. Justify Utterson's reluctance to read Lanyon's statement until after
   "the death or disappearance" of Jekyll.

9. What, in your opinion, did Utterson and Enfield see in Jekyll's face that so astounded or horrified them?

10. Could Dr. Jekyll's entire confession be written by Hyde? Explain.

ESSAY TOPICS

1. At the beginning of the novel, Dr. Jekyll is in total control of Mr. Hyde, yet at the end of the novel, Mr. Hyde is in control of Dr. Jekyll. Show how this reversal came about.

2. Utterson as a narrator is objective and honest, and yet he often comes to the wrong conclusion about matters such as forgery, Hyde's existence, Jekyll's motives, and other matters. Discuss the character of Utterson and how he is so often misled in his opinions.

3. Contrast Dr. Jekyll and Dr. Lanyon in their basic responses to scientific medicine, to metaphysics, to the basic nature of evil itself, and to man's duality.

4. Discuss this novel as a "mystery story" and demonstrate how there are many clues that lead the reader to solve the "mystery" before the solution is revealed to us in the final chapters.

5. Using this novel as your basis, discuss the nature of "good" and "evil," or "the double" and the duality of man's nature, as presented in this novel.

6. What qualities does Utterson possess that allow so many prominent men (Jekyll, Lanyon, Sir Danvers, etc.) to trust him so completely?

7. Why is the novel more effective by having all the main characters – Utterson, Jekyll, Lanyon (and maybe Enfield and Sir Danvers) – be prominent, well known, respected men?

8. There are many narrators – among them, Enfield, Utterson, Poole, Lanyon, and Jekyll – in this novel. Discuss what each narrator contributes to the novel.

SELECT BIBLIOGRAPHY

CHESTERTON, G. K. *Robert Louis Stevenson*. London, 1927.

DONAN, DOYLE, A. *Through the Magic Door*. London, 1907.

COOPER, LETTICE. *Robert Louis Stevenson*. Edinburgh and London, 1899.

DAICHES, DAVID. *Robert Louis Stevenson*. Glasgow, 1947.

EIGNER, EDWIN M. *Robert Louis Stevenson and Romantic Tradition*. Princeton, 1966.

ELWIN, MALCOLM. *The Strange Case of Robert Louis Stevenson*. London, 1950.

FIEDLER, LESLIE. *No! in Thunder*. London, 1963.

GROSS, JOHN. *The Rise and Fall of the Man of Letters*. London, 1969.

GUTHRIE, CHARLES. *Robert Louis Stevenson*. Edinburgh, 1920.

HELLMAN, GEORGE. "The Stevenson Myth," *Century Magazine*, December 1922.

HINKLEY, LAURA. *The Stevensons: Louis and Fanny*. New York, 1950.

OSBOURNE, LLOYD. *An Intimate Portrait of R. L. S.* New York, 1924.

SMITH, JANET ADAM. *Henry James and Robert Louis Stevenson*. London, 1948.

STEPHEN, LESLIE. *Robert Louis Stevenson*. London, 1903.

NOTES

NOTES

NOTES

NOTES

Made in the USA
San Bernardino, CA
24 June 2020

74253454R00038